W9-AEY-408

"Many books have been written on the remediation of learning disabilities, but this one is unique in its attempt to categorize each problem into definition, manifestation, and educational approaches or techniques. . . . This is an excellent resource and reference work, it belongs on the shelf of all special education teachers."

Learning Disabilities
Handbook
for Teachers

Second Printing

Learning Disabilities Handbook for Teachers

Some Educational Disabilities Are Listed
with Definitions, Manifestations, and Remediations Explained
with a Survey of Some Teaching Materials
Commercially Produced and Available
in Stores and Instructional Material Centers

By

ROBERT B. BLACKWELL, Ed.D.

and

ROBERT R. JOYNT, Ed.D.

Special Education Division
Bowling Green State University
Bowling Green, Ohio

CHARLES C THOMAS • PUBLISHER
Springfield • Illinois • U.S.A.

Published and Distributed Throughout the World by

CHARLES C THOMAS • PUBLISHER

Bannerstone House

301-327 East Lawrence Avenue, Springfield, Illinois, U.S.A.

© *1972, by* CHARLES C THOMAS • PUBLISHER

ISBN 0-398-02234-8

Library of Congress Catalog Card Number: 72-169871

First Printing, 1972

Second Printing, 1976

*With THOMAS BOOKS careful attention is given to all details of
manufacturing and design. It is the Publisher's desire to present books that are
satisfactory as to their physical qualities and artistic possibilities and
appropriate for their particular use. THOMAS BOOKS will be true to those
laws of quality that assure a good name and good will.*

Printed in the United States of America

RN-10

PREFACE

IT is not our objective to give a definitive answer for every educational failure or every physical disability. This monograph was written as a reference or resource for teachers to use to attain a more complete understanding and delineating of learning disorders so that further resource may be elicited for impingement for supportive or remedial amelioration.

It is important to consider, when reading literature dealing with remedial education, that the human body is a complex organism, with the brain the most intricate organ of all, with millions of factors which affect the total organism's adequate and acceptable function. With this in mind, it is possible that no diagnosis is ever wholly correct. Many hidden and unseen factors may be at work clouding the real issues. Physical disabilities are obvious if the handicap is visually observable, i.e. amputations, sightless eyes, mongolism, or severe body tremors. But some disabling and handicapping conditions such as mental retardation, hearing loss, or eye imperfections may only be revealed by expert diagnosticians.

In the screening of children with physical and psychological problems, teachers are often handicapped not only in identifying the problem by name but also in providing or suggesting immediate educational planning. It is not uncommon in many school districts to encounter difficulty in finding assistance in identification, physical diagnosis, psychological evaluation, or educational planning for children with learning problems. Even in districts where these services are available, waiting lists are extensive and help is frustratingly difficult to procure. In the meantime, the child is in the classroom and becomes an increasing and often disturbing concern to both himself and the teacher. Initiative, therefore, lies with the teacher not only in referral but in attempting formal educational procedures until help comes.

v

With the limited assistance offered by most administrative personnel, the teacher is often left having to be the only person working with the child for extensive periods.

It is hoped that this publication might serve as a reference in giving the teacher not only a resource of things to do but also a bibliography for further reading and study to maintain and improve teaching approaches. It is still recognized that the classroom teacher is the most important ingredient in a child's educational process. Research tends to suggest that the experienced observant classroom teacher is often the best source of diagnostic understanding of educational needs of children.

There are a number of schools of thought on remedial approaches to learning disabilities. Some of these have little validated research. Care should be taken in accepting a single method as "guaranteed" to remediate a learning disability. A wide variety of materials should be tried under objective circumstances before a decision is reached as to the worth of the method. We believe that there are severe disabilities which can usually be helped but cannot be "cured" by any treatment or method now known. One of the most criminal indulgences any remediator can perform is to offer parents a "sure cure" through a particular method of treatment. It is suspected that the intimate-accepting skilled therapist may be the most important ingredient in the treatment milieu.

ACKNOWLEDGMENTS

W E want to thank Mrs. B. McMillin for allowing us to use the Instructional Media Center, and also Miss Susan Canavino and Timothy Allison for their assistance in examining and rating the materials from the Center.

R.B.B.
R.R.J.

CONTENTS

Learning Disabilities
Handbook
for Teachers

I

VISION AND VISUAL
MOTOR DISABILITIES

THIS section consists of a delineation of problems which arise out of situations involving visual and motor coordination. These problems are thought to develop as a result of poor training, slow maturation, or minimal brain dysfunction. A teacher's knowledge in the areas of vision and motor function will enable him to have a more comprehensive approach to remediation of such learning impediments.

EYE MOVEMENT

Definition

Vision is also measured in eye movement. Measurement of the extent and kind of movement can be made by having the child follow a penlight or object through various quadrants of movement.

Manifestations

Eye movement problems are seen in children who constantly lose their place while reading. Usually they keep their finger on the page and read in unusual rhythms. Eye movements may be seen as jerky, clumsy, or incoordinate.

Educational Approaches or Techniques

This disability may involve physical as well as experiential deprivations. Some of the following might be tried:

1. Eye movement may be involved in problems of readiness which could occur from a lack of preparatory experiences. The child has not had experience in following structured stimuli.

2. The teacher can require the student to follow objects or to attend to stimuli on specific direction, e.g. having a child follow a lit object in left-to-right orientation, looking at near and far objects on command. This can also be done in other spatial spheres.

3. Use overlay cut-out forms and move them along reading lines.

4. The tachistoscope, which may be homemade or purchased, can be used to focus eye movement.

5. Even flash cards are a method of eye movement control.

6. A series of booklets called "tracking books" are engineered for teaching correct eye movement.

Eye movement problems of a clinical nature, i.e. stuttering eyes, should be referred for medical investigation. Until definite diagnosis is obtained, visually demanding materials should be avoided.

EYE-TEAM COORDINATION

Children may lose interest in seeing tasks and/or depend highly on listening skills. Deviation of the eye may result in the development of peculiar head-holding positions, lack or "looking you in the eye", and other peculiarities of fixation

Clinical problems, again, should be referred to an ophthalmologist of competency in areas related to other than a disease model.

Again eye-team skills may be a matter of readiness, and material detailed in current educational literature may be

Any problem where the two eyes do not perform as one is eye-team coordination. The eyes turn in opposition to each other or one may drift from a focus.

Definition

Terms used to describe this problem are strobismus, tropia, wall-eye, squint, cast, "lazy eye," amblyopia, and hypertiopia; all mean nonalignment of the visual axis.

Manifestations

that only serve to increase psychic disturbances and to impede good interpersonal relationships.

Educational Approaches or Techniques

employed. Frostig, Kephart, and others have extensive exercises in these areas which overlap with eye-hand coordination and eye movement skills.

EYE-HAND COORDINATION

This is explained in greater detail under "Motor Impairment." A brief description is given here. Eye-hand coordination is sometimes described as the process of being able to take a stimuli in through the eye, having it processed by the brain and passed into the hand in a motor function.

Problems occur for the child in accurate discrimination of, and location of, objects in space. The child is unable to accurately duplicate drawings or to position objects. In some instances, the child will state that the replication is accurate and in other cases will say it is not but will be unable to correct it on demand. Placing parquet blocks of varied colors in designs is a good test of

Eye-hand coordination should involve a good physical or motor program. As skills are gained in total motor areas, the entire body becomes a supporting and contributing action system for the interpretation and comprehension of the symbols of the classroom. Some activities to build this skill are as follows:

1. Any type of activity involving the hands with vision, in either a gross or fine motor action, will contribute to coordination.
2. Right-left, up-down, and clock-

wise-counterclockwise concepts may all be introduced and involve the child's entire body. Changes in directions will also add to coordination.

3. Chalkboard routines with children showing bilateral circles, horizontal lines, vertical lines, or following dots will also contribute to improvement in eye-hand skills.

Also refer to Frostig, Kephart, Lippencott, and Continental Press Materials.

eye-hand coordination. Children usually have trouble batting balls or catching thrown objects and may assume a stance of arms extended and feet wider apart when playing games requiring catching.

VISUAL FORM PERCEPTION

This is inadequate visual perception of objects or forms.

The relation of visual imagery in interpreting primary experiences to the pictures and words in a printed classroom book are commonly seen in children experiencing poor memory and/or an inability to attend to details. Letter-form and/or letter-sequence rever-

Visual form perception is not expected to be performed with proficiency prior to the second or third grade. Research tends to indicate that children who are unable to acquire visual form perception skills by the third grade often have difficulty in all academic areas, particularly in spelling and writing. Too often, teachers seeing a child with visual form

Definition

Manifestations

sals are also common with this disorder. Children with this disorder, when asked to explain what is on a printed page, will sometimes say a group of words jumbled or piled up. Others may see wide spaces between lines or words. Trouble in comparison of shapes and forms is also evidence of this disability.

Educational Approaches or Techniques

problems are inclined to have the child involved in repetitive practice of symbols and forms themselves rather than using underlying processes of eye-hand coordination and eye movement skills. The teacher may use many different methods in the classroom, such as:

1. Flash cards (letters, words, sentences).

2. Tachistoscope (commercial products or homemade), providing a flashing of symbols so as to help the student improve their visual imagery of the symbols.

3. Space-writing—quick visual presentation of symbols; students draw in the air what they remember.

4. Chalkboard work.

5. Student writing symbol, erasing, writing a certain number of times, and drawing again (recommend starting with figures, then letters,

and then finally words and sentences).

6. Templates of geometric forms, letters, and words; student traces over such templates, erases these, and waits a certain period of time and rewrites from memory.

REFRACTION

Refraction refers to disorders of focal distances as nearsightedness and farsightedness. Distortions or inadequacies can so alter the comprehension process that it may void the auditory and tactile comprehension signals. Squinting, blinking, and holding material at close focal distances, deterioration of reading ability, and reading progress deterioration are a few of the signs of refractive problems.

The size and shape of the eyeball determines the refractive error, which in turn determines the need for glasses. In farsightedness (hyperopic) the image comes into focus behind or in back of the retina. In nearsightedness (myopic), the image comes in focus in front of the retina. Glasses can accommodate this malfunction of focus. In

Refractive problems are mainly problems that need to be clinically evaluated. These are visual problems that a competent ophthalmologist can diagnose, and he can make proper recommendations. The teacher should be aware of the clinical manifestations that indicate such difficulties, such as a student's avoidance of visual tasks, fatigue, squinting, blinking, rubbing of eyes, etc. The teacher may aid such a student until corrective measures are obtained by:

1. Reducing periods of visual stimulation.

Definition	Manifestations	Educational Approaches or Techniques
astigmatism, there is an irregular focus, so there may be more than one area of focus.		2. Assigning other students to read to the individual. 3. Providing rest periods for such students. 4. Using other sense modalities for instruction (e.g. auditory, tactile with tapes, records, etc.) In conclusion, the teacher trains himself to be aware of clinical manifestation of such problems, know whom to refer such students to, and provide adequate follow-up for such a problem in the classroom.

VISUAL PERCEPTION REVERSALS AND INVERSIONS

Definition	Manifestations	Educational Approaches or Techniques
The student, when confronted with the task of reproducing visual stimuli by writing, reverses or inverts a letter, letters, or	The classic manifestation of such a problem is found in the reversal of such letters as d's to b's or g's to p's and in seeing such words as "saw" for	The causes for such a problem may be (a) Poor left-right discriminations, (b) poor eye-hand coordination, (c) confused dominance of eye, hand, etc., and (d) immaturity of the visual neurological

whole words. These reversals or inversions are expressed by students in varrying frequency. This problem may occur at one time and not at another time. This problem is most frequently expressed by young children but may be one that lasts a lifetime. To assume that a student will "outgrow" such a deficiency in his visual and motor understanding is not a fair evaluation of the problem. A systematic and regular program of remediation is necessary.

"was" and "no" for "on." This problem may also show up in figure drawings, map work, and any other representation that has to do with a visual presentation. However, the problem will most often be recognizable in exercises dealing with the visual copying of letters and words.

system.

Correction of such a problem can be aided by the following activities:

1. Tracing of letters and words (Fernald approach).

   a. Have the student trace with his finger the confused letter or word. This tracing may be done on many different surfaces, and it is often best for the student to use different and varied surfaces. The tactile sensation hopefully will stimulate visual and tactile memorization of the proper presentation of the letter or word.

   b. Have the student, during the tracing process, say the letter or word.

   c. Have the student then reproduce from memory what he has felt, seen, and stated.

2. Teaching left to right discrimination.

Definition	Manifestations	Educational Approaches or Techniques
		a. Have the student use his finger or some other object to move along under the words and sentences he is reading. This method will hopefully improve the student's habit of left-to-right eye movements as well as improving his concentration on letters and words.
		3. Teaching concentration for letters.
		a. Have the student read through a mixed group of letters, checking off the letters of the alphabet in proper order. He may only cross out a "b" after he has crossed out an "a" and only as he moves visually from left to right across each line (e.g. of one line, g,c,a̸,d,b̸).
		4. Teaching visual concentration.
		a. Have the student use a flash process where he is expected to

state with accuracy the letters and words as they are quickly presented to him. This type of exercise can be provided by the use of simple flash cards and of more expensive commercially purchased machines.

DEGREES OF VISUAL ACUITY

Blindness is defined as a central visual acuity of 20/200 or less in the better eye with correcting glasses; or central visual acuity of more than 20/200 if there is a field defect in which the peripheral field has contracted to such an extent that the widest diameter of visual field subtends an angular distance no greater than 20 degrees.

Partially sighted would refer

Vision is also measured in peripheral as well as central acuity.

The totally blind student can best be served in a special school for early training. If the child is bright and well motivated, he may survive in a regular high school with assistance from a reader, talking books, and braille material.

Partially-sighted students will benefit from proper lighting, magnifiers, and preferential seating in the classroom. It has been found that children with partial vision do not strain their eyes with proper lighting and magnification. Many

Definition	*Manifestations*	*Educational Approaches or Techniques*
	to any degree of disability between 20/200 and average vision of 20/20 with corrective lenses.	standard textbooks are now printed in large type for visually handicapped persons.

INFECTIOUS DISEASES OF THE EYE

Definition	*Manifestations*	*Educational Approaches or Techniques*
Infectious diseases refer to diseases of the eye and its structures, including the lids, lacrimal system, conjunctiva, cornea, sclera, and uvea.	This may be evident in easily discerned infections such as "pink eye," but also can be subtle inner-eye anomalies requiring an ophthalmologist for detection.	Infectious diseases are treated only by members of the medical profession. The teacher's responsibility here is to be aware of such problems and follow through with referral to the proper medical personnel. If medication is to be taken by the student, it should be the teacher's responsibility to find out what it is and make sure that the student, during school hours, takes such prescribed medication. Early observation and treatment may prevent infections from spreading.

FORM CONSTANCY

Definition

Form constancy occurs if forms or shapes do not remain constant and the child cannot recognize them. Even slight changes remove the ability of the individual to see similarities. It appears that similarities of shape, size, and color are not recognized as relationships.

Manifestations

In addition to indiscrimination of shape, size, and color of objects, words, when put into new context, are not recognized. A general inability to transfer learned skill to new material is often found.

Educational Approaches or Techniques

Form constancy problems may be more common among children who receive little environmental stimulation. Early use of some of the following may assist children with this disability.

1. Early training should be started, using three-dimensional materials or objects, with the child discriminating likes and differences.

2. In reading, care should be taken to be consistent in the form used, both in presentation and in printed words.

3. New forms should gradually be introduced.

4. Careful use of written symbols and words should be made to adhere to a consistent form.

5. A linguistic approach of use of I.T.A. (Initial Teaching Alphabet)

Definition	Manifestations	Educational Approaches or Techniques
		is advised.
		Resources for reading in this area are the books of Getman, Smith, Kephart and Frostig.

PERCEPTUAL PROBLEMS WITH FIGURE GROUND DISTRACTIBILITY

Definition	Manifestations	Educational Approaches or Techniques
This child cannot keep his attention on a fixed point without interference from distracting stimuli. He is unable to focus his attention on a specific item at will.	This disability is often noticed in clumsy, inconsistent, confused behavior. In reading, the child constantly loses his place and has difficulty finding it again without help. It also may be reflected in an inability to hold attention on words or to perform word blending and syllabication.	Educational approaches could include some of the following: 1. Written material should be free of confusing background, i.e. poorly erased blackboards. 2. Writing should be extra large. 3. Pages should contain few illustrations and widely spaced lines and words. 4. The child is permitted to hold line being read by using a plain card or cut-out template. 5. Instructional periods should be interspersed with activity periods.

6. A very effective way of dealing with this problem is by outlining the figure presentation in a dark color. In this way, the central visual cue is highlighted for the reader.

SPATIAL RELATIONSHIP

Spatial relationship is associated with an inability to see the relationship between two objects as they relate to self and to each other.

The child has, for instance, failure in sequential tasks and cannot string beads according to an example. He may confuse letters in writing and numbers in arithmetic. He may see symbols jumbled, reversed, or in random order.

Children may be helped with some combination of the following suggestions:

1. Practice comparing forms, starting with three-dimensional large objects and working to single-dimensional small objects.

2. Do work with semi-abstractions, using color coding with forms as well as shapes and then move to abstraction of writing and arithmetic symbols.

3. Maze-type exercises have been found useful—either those suggested by Frostig of following dots or other types with number

Definition	Manifestations	Educational Approaches or Techniques
		sequence or those found in the Weschler Intelligence Scale for Children (WISC).
		4. Memory practice by reproducing forms from memory should be tried with constant reinforcement with the correct form.
		The chief describer of this disability has been Frostig.

POSITION IN SPACE

Definition	Manifestations	Educational Approaches or Techniques
Position in space is associated with an incomprehension of objects or the placing of objects in relation to self. A lack of basic knowledge of left and right and a confusion of the two are usually found.	This disability is accompanied with an inability and confusion in placing objects from verbal directions: confusing left and right; reversal of letters such as b and d, etc., which are also reversed in reading; and substitutions in reading, as well as difficulty in	This disability is initially dealt with in a gross-motor way. Later, as skills improve, it may be brought to a pencil and paper semi-abstract media. Early training should include some of the following:
		1. A variety of body-awareness activities should be planned, in which body orientation and right and left are emphasized.

working with initial sounds.

2. Children should be encouraged to play marching games and body-part identification emphasizing left and right.

3. Allow children to write and draw on the board.

4. Use of large print and writing seems to work well.

5. Use of the vocabulary of spatial orientation, i.e., on, under, above, over, etc. should be gone through with the child, demonstrating his comprehension of each concept.

Frostig and Kephart have the most extensive material dealing with remediation of this disability.

II

EMOTIONAL AND SOCIAL DISABILITIES

Disabilities described in this section are of wide variety and usually arise from environmental factors. Some emotional disability may arise from genetic origins, but most handicaps attributed to genetic causes are in question.

A knowledge of the home environment, siblings, and emotional milieus surrounding the child will enable the teacher to evaluate behavior.

FAILURE TO COMPLETE ASSIGNMENTS

Definition	*Manifestations*	*Educational Approaches or Techniques*
This is a student's inability to follow through on school-related assignments.	This type of student manifests such behavior by: 1. Never turning in school work. 2. Turning in school work that is partially completed. 3. Spending a great deal of time daydreaming, dawdling, and playing. 4. Uses a great number of excuses for not completing assignments. 5. Spending a great deal of his time moving from task to task without finding any satisfaction in completion.	In many of these cases, an understanding of the student's home situation is advisable. The aid of a psychologist or home visitor may help in determining the home's influence upon the problem and may result in recommendations for adjustments in parental handling of the child. The following are recommendations that can be used in the home and at school: 1. Establish definite goals for the student pertaining to each lesson or task. These goals need to be within the ability of the student. 2. Follow through on each lesson or task, making sure that the student has completed the assignment. This may take longer periods of

Definition	Manifestations	Educational Approaches or Techniques
	These are some reasons for such difficulties. These are 1. Psychological problems. 　a. Anxiety resulting in hyperactivity. 　b. Parental conflicts—punishment by parents or authority figure. 　c. Lack of secure feelings—more comfortable in fantasy work. 　d. Ego strengths—lacks confidence in one's work. He is unwilling to try or to complete (failure-avoider). 2. Management problems. 　a. Parents and/or teachers may not follow through with proper demands.	time than had been previously required. At this point, the time element is not as much of a concern as is the element of completeness. 3. Reward successful completion with a rewarding system that the student has established. This should involve rewards that are meaningful to the student. 4. Relieve pressures of constant verbal probing. Often this type of approach only increases the problem. You should be firm but with a minimum of verbal communication.

b. Parents have always given into the child, letting him do what he wants (spoiled child).

c. Parental pressures have been so great that the child flees from the responsibilities of school.

PERFECT INDIVIDUAL

Definition

The perfect individual is the student who feels that he must always be perfect in behavior, school work, and social interaction.

Manifestations

The manifestations of such a student's behavior are shown by his compulsive drive to do all or one of the following:

1. Have such behavior that the teacher will never need to correct him.
2. Complete his school work in such a manner

Educational Approaches or Techniques

The teacher, in handling such students, should be concerned with the behavior and not treat such problems lightly. An individual's need to be perfect in an imperfect world can lead to more serious emotional problems as he grows older. Often teachers either neglect or reinforce such "goody, goody" attempts at perfection. Students should be taught to strive

Definition

Manifestations

Educational Approaches or Techniques

that there will be no errors.

3. Have such interpersonal relationships with his peers that there are never any quarrels, fighting, or general negative interruption of a normal relationship.

This type of student will become upset when any of the above needs are not met. His desire for perfection in these areas will leave him frustrated and greatly anxious when he is not able to achieve such perfect behavior. This anxiety may be shown by crying, nervousness, tics, and other inappropriate adjustments to such a situation.

towards perfection but that this may be a goal seldom achieved.

A teacher may take the following course of action, depending on the assumed course of the behavior:

1. Change in Teacher-pupil relationship. Pressure by the teacher should be avoided in demanding perfect or near-perfect school work. A teacher must be willing with such a student to settle for less than his (best) potential, knowing that his (best) potential is too often achieved with a more damaging emotional health problem. Such examples of this would be to ease up on grading his papers (forget grades), lessen assignments, requirements, tolerate mistakes without commenting, etc.

2. Teacher-pupil counseling. Take time to discuss his problems with

the student, attempt to point out their individual nature and involve his need system, which may be unrealistic. Explain that the vast majority of people in our society do not demand such exacting behavior in any area. The teacher should be open and not "tell" but discuss and, most important, listen.

3. Teacher-parent counseling. If the teacher feels that the pressure is from the home and in most of these cases this will be found to be true, parent counseling is necessary. The parents should be "informed" of the *observed* behavior of their child and the perfectionist attitude of their child. A more permissive attitude should be allowed at home freeing the student from the pressures of such exacting behavior. A parent should come to realize that chil-

Definition	Manifestations	Educational Approaches or Techniques
		dren need lots of room for error, as this is what makes for healthy adult adjustment.
		In conclusion, one of the most important things that a teacher can do for such a student is to show appreciation for this student as an individual, regardless of the type of performance he achieves. The teacher accepts him as a unique individual first and as a student second.

PHOBIC REACTION

Definition	Manifestations	Educational Approaches or Techniques
Phobic reaction is a syndrome characterized by the presence of one or more phobias.	These are exaggerated fears of something in the environment and they stem from unconscious emotional problems. They have sometimes been labeled the "normal neuroses of childhood" . in that they occur in almost every child in	There are certain approaches that may work with these children. However, in the case of a deep-seated phobic reaction, professional counseling is recommended. 1. Psychoanalytically many of these fears are thought to derive from unresolved conflicts with the parental

the ages of three to five years. Typical examples are fear of dogs, the dark, heights, or mythical characters such as monsters or witches. Transient phobias can be disregarded in early childhood and will usually disappear as the child enters his pre-teen years. Those children needing special help will have phobias which are more prolonged, more numerous, or more exaggerated than normal. In order to qualify as a phobia, a fear must have an exaggerated character which exceeds realistic expectations. Because of this, it is almost necessary for severe cases to be referred for psychiatric assistance.

figures and therefore cannot be treated without involving the parents.

2. In some instances, especially fear of injury or illness, it may be thought by the child to be punishment for forbidden impulse toward some loved person. If the teacher maintains a professional, objective, but accepting role with his children, difficulties of this nature may not arise.

3. Teachers must use professional nonreinforcing attitudes toward children seeking reinforcement for psychosomatic reactions. This does not mean that there is no place for sympathy or empathy but only no place for maudlin smothering.

4. Success has been obtained in reducing fears by a method called "desensitizing." In cases of phobias about animals, this is accomplished by handling a piece of fur, then a stuffed toy, before exposure of the child to a live animal. Rewarding the child with

Definition	Manifestations	Educational Approaches or Techniques
		food or candy on an acceptable response to his phobia is appropriate.
		5. School phobias are usually related to an overprotective mother who might disappear if the child separates himself from her by going off to school. These mothers have usually shown ambivalence of love and hostility toward the child, and as a consequence, the child lacks basic trust. A teacher can help by making the school an interesting place with many diversified interests, and by getting the mother to seek professional help. The teacher should be sure to treat phobic children with acceptance and consistency. Curing school phobias may also require the teacher to force the mother to leave the child without concerns or verbal reinforcement of her love for the child or her reassurance of nonabandonment.

DAYDREAMING

Definition

Daydreaming is losing contact with the present. This may also be called disassociation (common among teachers at boring faculty meetings).

Manifestations

The child may stare into space, sit with eyes closed, or, under some conditions, rotate the head or other part of the body in ritualistic, repetitious movement. This behavior is considered serious when it becomes prolonged or persists over periods of time, and when it interferes with the reception of verbal or auditory stimuli.

Educational Approaches or Techniques

The behavior may be considered by some psychologists to be a withdrawal from an uncomfortable world into a safer imaginary state. Within the state, the child may be able to gain pleasure, as well as revenge, in fantasy thought. Whenever the classroom becomes cluttered with excessive demands or threats, the withdrawal into fantasy will occur. Remediation of this condition may be helped by:

1. Reducing the amount of demands at any one time.
2. Gearing tasks to the child's individual needs of accomplishment, including many successes.
3. Reducing tasks to simple terms, and giving them to the child one at a time in short, rewarding intervals.

Definition

Manifestations

Educational Approaches or Techniques

4. Placing the child near the teacher's desk where maximum stimuli is originating.

5. Standing next to the child when giving direction and physically touching the child during the direction giving.

6. Emphasizing each word of the instruction being given by tapping the rhythm out on the child's arm or hand as the words are stated.

7. Compounding directions and tasks gradually.

8. Using learning situations in which the child participates through movement or gross motor usage, such as doing work at the board or chart.

9. Forcing the child to maintain eye contact while the teacher is giving directions This may

entail placing the hand under the child's chin and elevating his head until eye contact is made.

10. This disassociative behavior is indicative of an emotional problem and should be referred to experts for further diagnosis and treatment. Accepting the child and positively approving correct responses may reward him to the point where he will want to please the teacher by remaining alert and present-oriented.

11. Assigning another child in the class to tutor this child would help if some of the disassociation is the result of antagonism to adult authority figures.

IMPULSIVITY

Definition

An impulse is an automatic process without conscious thought involved. Reactions may be in acting out antagonistic feelings or in defensive, protective, or withdrawal behavior. Usually impulsivity is seen as action without thinking, demanding immediate attention.

Manifestations

The impulsive child is seen as acting out in usually a negative act, i.e. such as suddenly reacting to another child in hitting or throwing things. Actions are usually immediate and are, perhaps, a subconscious demand for immediate attention. The child may be found to be an overly worried, highly anxious child who reacts too quickly and too much to stimuli. The major suggestion is that these are a result of few inner controls functioning and that the learned behavior is not governed by conscious thought.

Educational Approaches or Techniques

Suggested procedures for handling the child may include any or all of the following:

1. Show positive acceptance of warmth and understanding. Do not use a negative approach.

2. Provide a structured, consistent environment.

3. Be sure the child knows the behavioral limits, and provide a constancy of these perimeters.

4. Have patience and give persistent reminders to the child that he is not the only one and that all actions must be preceded by thought.

5. Tasks should be designed with the childs ability in mind so that he gets the reassurance of acceptance through successful experiences.

6. Care should be taken to avoid his becoming overdependent because of too much guidance and supervision.

DEVIATION FROM SEXUAL NORMS

Children who can readily be identified as deviating from the sexual norms are not commonly identified at the elementary school level. Feminine boys and masculine girls may be one mode of norm deviation, as well as either acting out sexual curiosity or having a preoccupation with sex interests.

Elementary school methods of acting out sexual curiosity may vary from the "skirt flipper" and "doctor examiner" to the sixth grade "make-out." Early maturity may bring on adult figures, dress, and actions, especially in girls. Some girls may be only the victims of overambitious mothers. Genital handling may arouse anxiety in parents and children, especially if it persists through the lower grades.

Cases of sexual inversion are best diagnosed and handled by experts. Teachers may consider some of the following suggestions helpful.

1. Although sex information is becoming more readily available, it is still a taboo subject in many schools. A careful check of school policy would be suggested before the teacher attempts to deal with sex instruction.

2. The giving out of specific information and appropriate terms will depend greatly on the ability of the child to absorb the information given. It is important not to underestimate a child's concern,

Definition

Manifestations

Educational Approaches or Techniques

but at the same time, do not read into a child's remarks something he does not actually mean. Be objective.

3. "Skirt flipping" and behavior of this nature may only be a means of gaining attention. By doing this, a boy may receive the only attention a teacher gives him. Acceptance and attention at other times will help relieve some of the interest in this behavior. Conversation should be had with the child, and firm, friendly, objective limits should be explained to him and then enforced. If a number of parents become involved, a meeting with them may resolve some of the tensions by placing some of the responsibility for control of behavior in their hands. Care should be taken to keep the

meeting objective and without an attempt at assessing blame. The actions of all children are attempts to meet needs, however, inappropriate.

4. Early maturation, especially in girls, may throw them out of step with their peers. The girl should be able to converse with significant adults to interpret how she feels. Meeting the girl's need for male companionship and close supervision during her developmental period will help her through this stage satisfactorily. Effort should be made to help her with personal grooming and appearance, so that her general impressions are appropriate.

5. Corrective measures should be kept at a very low pressure when dealing with masturbation. In smaller children, the use of interesting, two-handed tasks may be a

Definition	Manifestations	Educational Approaches or Techniques
		solution. Masturbation will usually occur when classwork becomes difficult, creating anxiety and tension. Clothes should be checked for being tight and uncomfortable. If the situation cannot be alleviated in spite of all effort on the part of the teacher, professional help should be sought.

6. Children who exhibit inappropriate sex roles need strong, adequate sex models. This may mean changing a child's class, obtaining a "Big Brother or Sister," or bringing the child into contact with a significant figure within the home, community or school. Forcing a child to enter into activities considered "suitable" for his sex may serve only to push him further from the desired goal. Reinforcing by praise and rewards when he enters into

activities suitable for his sex is a way of modifying behavior. Hobby interests should be stressed, which are in keeping with proper sex roles. Activities which include both boys and girls may be the first step away from activities thought unsuitable for his sex.

7. The elimination of pornographic material is an important item to stress not only within the school but also the home. Much of a child's misinformation and preoccupation with sex come from influences of television, movies, and paperbacks.

8. Some of the most serious emotional disturbances found with children in psychiatric clinics involve sexual stimulations by adults. It may be that the child is sleeping in the same bed with an adult of the opposite sex or with both parents, or is being sexually

Definition	*Manifestations*	*Educational Approaches or Techniques*

STUTTERING

Definition

Stuttering is speaking with spasmodic repetition as a result of excitement or impediment.

Manifestations

Stuttering, a not-uncommon form of dyslalia (nonfluency), usually begins during childhood. Some speech pathologists prefer to separate it from stammering, which is defined as temporary periods of stuttering during the second, third, and fourth years of life. These are not unusual, due to the fact that some children's thoughts are formed faster than they can verbalize them. This usually occurs during periods when the child is in a

Educational Approaches or Techniques

manipulated by an adult. Changes in these situations probably require professional help and consultation.

In severe stuttering, the problem is believed to involve two major directions. First, the child has an emotional difficulty involving the handling of aggression; and second, he has channeled his difficulty into his organs of speech. The child has an emotional conflict about whether to be passive or aggressive. Stuttering represents the passive-aggressive dispute in which there is one impulse to speak and a passive impulse not to speak. Teachers may help in several ways:

1. The classroom should provide an unexciting, calm, accepting en-

hurry or excited. Serious stuttering is persistent, severe, and obvious; and although it is especially obvious during times when the child is excited, also appears when he is relatively calm.

vironment when the child is required to speak.

2. It may be necessary that psychotherapeutic measures be used to alleviate the fundamental emotional conflict of passive aggression.

3. Speech therapy is recommended to eradicate the habit patterns formed during the period of stuttering.

4. Teachers may offer opportunities to allow children to work off hostilities through active competitive sports.

5. Teachers should provide opportunities where this child can speak with little ego involvement but with feelings of success.

6. Acceptance of the child's speech is the key to his speech success—not necessarily perfect speech, but speech.

CHILD WHO STEALS

Definition

This student is one who has a need to possess property that belongs to others in the school.

Manifestations

The manifestations of this student's behavior are

1. Taking property that belongs to someone else when he assumes that no one can see him.
2. Taking property that belongs to someone else when that individual is present and aware of losing what is his.
3. Taking property that belongs to someone else and lacking the understanding that this property does not belong to him.

Educational Approaches or Techniques

The teacher, in handling such a student, usually does not solve such a problem by verbal and physical punitive means. If this is a deep-seated behavioral need, other approaches are recommended. The first step would be to determine the need that this student has for exhibiting such behavior. This is not always an easy task, as the student himself may not know the reasons for such behavior. There are a number of reasons, each of which may have to be dealt with in a different way.

1. The need for property taking (e.g. food, money). The student may be hungry or unable to maintain even his basic needs without obtaining things from other students. The teacher has the responsibility then to take action, if possible, to provide the basic wants

of such a child. This may mean having breakfast provided, lunch tickets, snacks, etc.; the contacting of agencies in the community for clothing, food allowances, etc.

2. The need to possess what others have, even though the object may be owned or purchased. Some of the psychological explanations for stealing are that the child learns by so doing that he will get attention, even though the attention is adverse. Another explanation is that it is an extreme need for affection, so he steals articles often of no value to possess—in a sense, a part of someone loved. **Strong acceptance and understanding are needed** to help the child realize that affection cannot be elicited in this fashion.

3. A teacher may provide small "love gifts" of unwanted jewelry, cosmetics, personal clothing, pencils, or other inexpensive items to prove to the child that he is accepted.

AUTISM

Definition	Manifestations	Educational Approaches or Techniques
Autism is considered to be a psychotic condition characterized by severe withdrawal from the environment. Another explanation is that it occurs in a person who cannot separate himself from his environment, and so he does not become a person but rather a "thing" or object like other objects or "things" in the surroundings.	One of the earliest identified manifestations is when a child fails to make the usual anticipatory movements prior to being picked up. When a child or youngster is picked up, he does not accommodate his body to the position in which he is being held. The child remains stiff and does not relax or accommodate by leaning into or fitting the body curves of the one holding him. Usually there are histories of prolonged rocking and head banging, obsessive interest in certain toys, repetitive and ritualistic play, often walking on tiptoe, inability to make direct verbal contact, insist-	Autism is described as the most baffling of the behavior disorders. Any traditionally oriented academic-task approach to teaching the youngsters would be unproductive. Application of operant conditioning procedures is the choice for modification of behavior problems. Complete cooperation of all persons coming in contact with the child must be enforced. First priorities in modification are directed toward extinction of behaviors such as self-destruction, tantrums, eating problems, etc. It is not known to what extent the behavioral defects observed in autistic children represent a basic constitutional or psychological defect. It is suggested that autism is a result of early maternal deprivation, and often treatment is involved with a warm, affectionate person giving a great deal of

"tender, loving care." It is not thought that any academic tasks should be attempted until these trys at behavior change are successful. In fact, these children would not respond successfully to academic tasks in any case. Because of the severity of this disorder, it is felt that few teachers should attempt to maintain a child of this disability in a school room. It is felt that it is even detrimental to this type of child to maintain him in a school classroom. Even on a one-to-one relationship with a trained psychologist, work with these children has resulted in frustrations with slow, difficult, and, in some instances, no, progress. The psychotic nature of the disability calls for experienced, trained help with extensive background in the psychology of behavior disorders. It would be suggested, however, that many of the references on behavior modification could be read for help in the changing of individual and group behavior which is detri-

ence in being left alone, repetition of nonsensical phrases or television commercials and other bizarre or inappropriate responses.

Definition	*Manifestations*	*Educational Approaches or Techniques*

Educational Approaches or Techniques (continued from previous)

mental to maintaining an academic setting conducive to learning. The teacher who is involved with such a child should refer him to special clinics offering proper diagnosis and treatment.

DISINHIBITION

Definition	*Manifestations*	*Educational Approaches or Techniques*

Disinhibition is sometimes called impulsivity, and the two may be hard to differentiate because they are similar responses. Disinhibition is referred to as the inappropriate response to a situation through motor activity with seeming loss of control or suppression of impulse.

Situations are responded to in part, rather than there being an appraisal of the entire response situation, and then usually with inappropriate intensity. Usually the action defies insight as to the consequence at the time of commitment. Later, remorse and concern may become evident. Brain-injured children may seem incapable of controlling their responses to extraneous stimuli and attempt a large

Although this disability may require help from the discipline of psychology, some of the following may be helpful:

1. Remove external stimuli that cause the student to react inappropriately to the school situations.
2. Locked cupboards may be necessary to allow the limitation of stimuli. With these, the teacher can bring out only prescribed materials.
3. Opportunity should be provided for the student to express himself through physical activities. It may

be necessary to provide equipment for individual physical exercise or to allow this child to exercise at a time separate from other children.

4. Time should be scheduled for counseling the student to reduce his anxiety level which has an effect on his acting-out behavior. At the same time, this child needs to feel that he is a contributing and meaningful member of his class.

5. Experiences that provide success are suggested, and these will also relieve anxieties that are caused by failure.

6. Informing the child of his daily expectations and schedules will also cut down on anxiety.

7. Instructions given this type of child should be specific, and materials which exploit a purposeful motor reaction are recommended.

number of activities within a very short period of time.

DISORGANIZATION

Definition	*Manifestations*	*Educational Approaches or Techniques*
Disorganization is described as the inability to complete or to attend to the learning situation.	Child responses are usually random and meaningless. There is an inability to function productively with self-directed tasks. There appears to be an incapability of coordinating experience with evaluation and goal direction. Vagueness and confusion seem to be predominate when purposeful activity is undertaken. As a consequence, inflexibility comes into play as the child attempts to protect himself against environmental change.	Structure may not be the opposite of disorganization, so it may be necessary to concentrate on some of the following rather than structuring environments: 1. Break all tasks down into simple sequential steps. Keep the tasks simple and accomplish one step at a time. 2. Routine, with a very gradual addition of any change, will limit the tendency to be disorganized. 3. A decrease in visual and auditory stimulation within the classroom has proven successful. It might mean putting the student in a booth or office of his own. 4. Let the student work on assignments and materials that are interesting to him. 5. Use of concrete materials is sug-

gested. Toys or simple puzzles which can be checked by the child both kinesthetically and visually are helpful.

6. Education may gradually move from the simple concrete materials to semi-abstract, which depends on the visual sense for correction.

7. Regression may be prevented by introducing all new experiences after success experiences with old materials. Introduction of materials must be done slowly and methodically.

CATASTROPHIC REACTION

Catastrophic reaction is found in most psychological writings and is explained as a loss of control without apparent, warranted cause.

The reaction to some minor situation may have the appearance of rage, terror, grief, or a temper outburst. It might be that the collapse of controls may be a combination of frustration, anguish, or anger.

The teacher should try some of the following:

1. Seek both a physical and psychological exam to rule out organic or psychic trauma as contributing factors.

2. When the reaction occurs, it is

Definition

Manifestations

These persons are referred to as having tenuous controls on emotions and may overreact to emotionally laden situations.

Educational Approaches or Techniques

best to change the child's activity from the one in which the reaction occurred to a new one.

3. Sometimes a "quiet room" can be provided where the child may go until he can regain his composure.

4. A positive attitude of comfort and reassurance is found helpful, rather than one of criticism and punishment.

5. An environment free of anxiety situations or overstimulation is recommended.

6. If the cause of the reaction is perceived, reality therapy is a good approach, with someone pointing out in a calm manner that mistakes or errors are made by everyone and there is little cause for overconcern. This may alleviate some of the overreacting.

PROBLEMS OF RECALL

Definition

This problem often occurs with students who have average or above-average intellectual ability but still have problems of remembering enough of their academic learning to stay up with the rest of the class.

Manifestations

This type of student expresses such behavior by his: (a) inability to recall what was just spoken, written, or read and (b) inability to recall after a few days what was spoken, written, or read.

In both (a) and (b), the teacher should be sure that the student has had ample exposure to the information so that under normal circumstances, he should have recall of the information.

Educational Approaches or Techniques

There are many factors which contribute to this problem. The most serious are (a) emotional health, (b) maturation, (c) lack of proper training in this cognitive function, and (d) minimal brain dysfunction.

Following are a few classroom suggestions:

1. Emotional health. Many times students with this problem lack anxiety-free minds so that they cannot store information even of a short-term nature.

   a. Visiting teacher. If the problem is of a serious nature, the student should be provided with the opportunity to express his fears. A visiting teacher working with the student one or

Definition	Manifestations	Educational Approaches or Techniques
		two days a week can help anxiety patterns of the student.
		b. Own teacher. The teacher can provide time throughout the day to talk openly with the student. This time should be spent in letting the student feel free with the teacher and the school environment. The classroom teacher can work much like a visiting teacher in allowing the student to talk while he is engaged in some other activity (e.g. drawing and recess). The better the teacher-pupil relationship established, the less anxiety the student is liable to show in the classroom.
		c. Parent-Teacher Conference. If the anxiety is interfering with the student's progress, a talk

with the parents is important. They should seriously discuss the home situation and attempt to reduce or alleviate anxiety situations.

2. Motivation. Many students lack ability to retain information because of this lack of interest in what is happening in the classroom. Presentation of all classroom material should be motivating, but in some situations, it never seems to hold their interest. Some of the following could be used, although there are other approaches the teacher could use:

   a. Have a different twist to the lesson.

   b. Have the student use the lesson in any way that he desires, as long as he is getting the same material as the other students.

   c. Use other students to work with the less-motivated.

Definition

Manifestations

Educational Approaches or Techniques

    d. Models from school or outside world can help to interest students. These may be presented in story form, tapes, or pictures, or resource people may be brought in.

    e. Motivation should be first, academic learning second. This must be the approach with these students. Be flexible and creative.

3. These are students who have recall problems because of improper training in this cognitive area. The teacher should first of all determine in what particular area the student has a problem (e.g. printed symbols, spoken language).

    a. Printed symbols.

      1) Tachistoscope or flash method. The student sees,

thinks, responds. This may be done using letters, numbers, geometric shapes, objects, etc.

2) Symbol relationship. The positional placement of figures, preferably letters and numbers should be studied. The presentation is done with symbols in a certain order, and structure is to repeat them in their proper sequence.

3) Relationship. Have students associate symbols to objects (e.g. a group of cards, one with the names of famous men, the other with pictures of these famous men); have students study, then take a break, then recall relationship between the two sets of cards.

HYPERACTIVITY

Definition	Manifestations	Educational Approaches or Techniques
Hyperactivity, most commonly refers to the child who cannot sit still and is literally "climbing the walls." This would be a type of motor hyperactivity. Other types of hyperactivity may include responses to irrelevant stimuli or an inability to refrain from reacting to all stimuli usually in some motoric mode.	The child may not be able to attend to a task for any length of time. He may dash about wildly from stimuli to stimuli. Verbal hyperactivity may be manifest in the asking of many questions without waiting for answers or just talking incessantly.	The teacher should try some of the following: 1. Structure the learning situation so that the work area is uncluttered and the stimuli are limited. Creating a private office or cubicle is appropriate, with plain walls and with visual limitations from distracting stimuli. Auditory stimulation should be limited as much as possible. 2. The child should be doing purposeful tasks, within his limits for successful completion and, if possible, involving some motor activity. 3. Anxiety may be a factor in the hyperactivity, so the schedules and routines should be somewhat controlled and repetitive to pro-

vide a secure structured environment.

4. The establishment of a reward system for appropriate behavior has proven successful. The reward may be one minute of free play time for every ten minutes of appropriate behavior.

5. Punishment usually increases the hyperactivity, so it should be avoided by providing alternatives so that the child is not idle for extended periods during which he could get into trouble.

DISTRACTABILITY AND SHORT ATTENTION SPAN

This perhaps is two separate classifications:

1. Where the child is easily led away from the focus task by insignificant stimuli.

This may be seen as a child who is involved in everything going on in all parts of the room but who is not completing the task at hand. This child is distracted by any noise, motion, light, or color; this

Suggested remediative techniques might include:

1. Reducing stimuli in visual and auditory spheres. This may entail an isolation cubicle which can be made temporarily out of old refrigerator boxes.

Definition	Manifestations	Educational Approaches or Techniques
2. The child who may work at a task but only for short periods, and as a consequence, is unable to finish it.	may result in erratic learning approaches as well as the appearance of hyperactivity, making any educational goal difficult.	2. Have the child face blank walls with his back to other students.
		3. Avoid background noises as well as any flashing lights.
		4. Avoid exciting, noisy, or running games prior to periods of expected concentration.
		5. The teacher should stand in back of the student when giving instructions, forcing the child to concentrate on the focal task.
		6. The teacher should avoid glittering, dangling jewelry as well as bright colors in clothes or cosmetics. Solid colors appear to be less confusing to these children than bright plaids.
		7. Avoid putting the child in a position in which he has to overtry to accomplish.
		8. Education of other children in

the room to individual differences is suggested to keep the child from feeling pressures of being different.

9. Realistic educational goals should be established so that the child achieves

   a. Short-term success.
   b. Frequent encouragement.
   c. Avoidance of failure.
   d. Opportunities to have some freedom of movement at the end of successful task completion.

10. The teacher should be concerned and accept the role and responsibility of writing an individual teaching prescription for children of this behavior.

OBSESSIVE-COMPULSIVE

Definition	Manifestations	Educational Approaches or Techniques
Obsessive behavior is a repetitious, obsessive, bothersome thought. Compulsive behavior is repetitious, magical gestures.	Obsessive thoughts are repetitions which recur to the child in spite of his attempts to stifle them. These are often distasteful and may include hostile thoughts towards authority figures or idealogical standards. Compulsions are repetitions, magical gestures, or rituals to ward off unforeseen and unknown dangers. The child may avoid stepping on cracks in the sidewalk. He may not be able to walk by a picket fence without touching each picket. Often, obsessions and compulsions are allied to super-	The features of the personality of the compulsive child reveal he still retains the emotional attitudes of a toddler. Because these are unacceptable to adults, he develops defenses to keep these impulses from becoming conscious. Unconscious impulses are in one direction and his defenses develop characterological attitudes in the opposite direction. Origins of an obsessive-compulsive reaction in a child can usually be traced either to exaggerated parental laxity or to parental rigidity. Classroom suggestions include the following: 1. Severe cases should be referred for psychotherapeutic help where part of the treatment will be with the parents in providing them with

stitions. Compulsive children try valiantly to avoid displeasing adults and are usually model students.

2. The teacher can assist in providing acceptance without reinforcing poor habits.

3. Attempts should be made to allay fear-inducing situations while at the same time avoiding overprotection.

4. Class structure should allow for a predictable world of order.

5. Effort should be made to obtain spontaneous responses from the child rather than ritualistic ones. Reinforcing these responses will help in overcoming ritualistic types.

6. Gradual revelations of immature behavior may be approached during times when the child breaks his facade in temper displays, which may be the only deviation in an otherwise controlled behavior.

CONCRETE BEHAVIOR

Definition

Concrete behavior describes an inability to generalize or to see similarities between situations. The term is sometimes used in describing the inability of some emotionally disturbed children, as well as brain-injured children, to differentiate reality and fantasy. The brain-injured child is the most difficult to elicit change over short periods of therapy. Emotionally disturbed children will often change automatically when the basic disturbing factors are dealt with.

Manifestations

These children have difficulty in handling assignments that call for generalization of similar situations. Consequently, they often approach similar tasks as if each were a new experience that had no relationship to their past learning. The problem here is that the student has no ability to conceptualize similarities in his present learning situation to anything that he has previously learned. An example of this in beginning reading is the sentence "I saw a ball"; knowing the words "saw" and "ball" will not help him to treat this as similar to previous learning. He will approach this

Educational Approaches or Techniques

Children of this description function best when tasks are unvaried and consistent. This is not, however, the educational purpose of this child. Some helpful techniques are the following:

1. The use of variations in the introductions of new concepts will be easier than attempting to emphasize the changing of old patterns of behavior.

2. Games of categorization and grouping can be used effectively in teaching the child the principles, so that he can begin to grasp the fact that every situation is not unique, separate, and distinct.

3. Real-life-experience teaching is more effective than vicarious or abstract presentations.

4. Opportunity should be provided for the student to use his own ability in

sentence as if he has never known any of these words. Discriminations between fantasy and reality which should disappear at the age of six or seven will continue to persist. Brain-injured children may overreact to the more frightening parts of fairy tales.

grouping objects, ideas, or words in scrapbooks or files, or even on a bulletin board.

5. Games that call for naming things that are the "same" or "different" can be used.

6. Teachers can use such common examples as the fact that the children in the room are all children, but some are boys and some are girls. This can be used with a wide variety of concrete objects. Containers or even milk cartons of different designs may confuse the brain-injured child.

PERSEVERATION

Repetition of an activity or phrases after the meaning and purpose have ceased is typical of this disability.

This is often associated with a neurological handicap and is manifested in the form of mental rigidity or the inability to change from activity to activity. It is sometimes referred to as that of a needle stuck

There is little evidence to cause one to believe that the child derives satisfaction from perseverative activity. Although many young children tend to do perseverative activity, i.e. repeat phrases over and over or go through repeated ritualistic physical routines, they can

Definition

Manifestations

Educational Approaches or Techniques

or a broken record.

A child drawing a line across a paper may not be able to stop upon reaching the edge but continue off the edge of the paper and desk. An appropriate response for one question may be carried over and used for a response for the next question. The child may continue to bounce a ball after it becomes inappropriate

usually do so in a controlled rather than uncontrolled fashion. Educational procedure would be to provide experiences which will stimulate the child to perceive in a more organized way; this rules out any repetitive rote learning or work involving drill. Some activities along this line are as follows:

1. Strong auditory or visual stimuli will tend to break up perseverative tendencies.

2. Practice sessions should be offered in a variety of forms.

3. Perseverative oral behavior may be common and the teacher may find it appropriate to interrupt with nonrelated activity and return to the original problem at a later time.

4. The teacher may need to gently get the child to change perseverative oral behavior by interrupting

the child, placing her hand on the child's arm or shoulder, and questioning the child to elicit the next response.

5. Choral reading or oral reading with a good companion reader should be stressed.

6. Help the child to achieve immediate successes.

7. Force movement with a controlled-reader device.

8. Keep assignment short.

III

MEDICAL AND
PHYSIOLOGICAL DISABILITY

Disabilities in this section cover those which may have a physical origin and, in most cases, can or should be under medical supervision. Teachers should be cognizant of not only the disability but also the medical history and medication of these children. The knowledge of medical information will help the teacher evaluate behavior.

ASTHMA

Definition

An estimated 1,600,000 children under 16 in the U.S. suffer from asthma. In a 1961 survey, this chronic condition accounted for 22.9 per cent of lost time from school by children 6 to 16. Symptoms, besides labored breathing and coughing, may include itching, nasal blockage, postnasal drainage, headaches, wheezing and repeated infections.

Manifestations

Manifestation of this disability may take a wide variety of forms and, as a consequence, may be difficult to identify. Attacks of asthma may occur as a result of psychological factors such as talking in front of a group or fear of an impending test; or they may occur as an allergic reaction to chalkboard dust, overexertion, changes in weather or temperature, as well as a wide variety of other physiological and psychological events.

Educational Approaches or Techniques

Regardless of the cause of the disability, a teacher might benefit from using some of the following recommendations:

1. The asthmatic child may atempt to use his illness for immediate gain – to attract attention. The teacher should discourage this attitude.
2. Learning is facilitated when the child regards himself as normal. Every effort should be made to treat the child as normal.
3. If the teacher sees that a child has asthmatic attacks after being at the chalkboard or working in woodworking, etc., he should transfer the child to another activity. If the child wishes to have another try at the activity which apparently has made him ill, he

Definition

Manifestations

Educational Approaches or Techniques

should be allowed to do so after a wait of from three to four weeks.

4. The vast majority of children with asthma can and should take part in regular physical education activities. The teacher should judge participation by observation of the child's "allergic threshold." This may vary from day to day and could be dependent on emotional state, infections, overexercise, weather change, etc.

5. Teachers should be in contact with parents and alert parents if attacks occur in school.

6. Teachers should be allerted to the side effect of some of the drugs commonly used for asthma.

    a. Adrenalin® or ephedrine can stimulate a child who is already overstimulated. This may be evidenced by nervousness, talkativeness, or generally hyperactive behavior.

b. Theophylline, which can open up or dilate the bronchial tubes may cause side effects of nausea.

c. Barbiturates used in combination with the above may have a sedative effect or, paradoxically, a stimulating effect.

d. Anti-histamines, which can be used for accompanying upper respiratory allergies, frequently cause some drowsiness.

7. If an asthmatic child is not receiving medical treatment, his parents should be advised to consult with a physician. Under no circumstances should a teacher give medical advice.

8. *Severe* asthmatics tend to exhibit immature personality structures; for example, with poor sex-role identifications, and hysterical

Definition	Manifestations	Educational Approaches or Techniques
		reactions appear frequently. Meeting basic emotional needs is advised with as near-normal acceptance as can be maintained.

EPILEPSY

Definition	Manifestations	Educational Approaches or Techniques
Generally the assumption is that a seizure is always associated with the specific disorder of epilepsy. This assumption is not definitely true because there are many diseases in which seizures may be one of the symptoms, such as brain tumors, infections of the brain, and biochemical disorders. Dr. John Hulings Jackson, English Neurologist,	The greatest number of persons are afflicted with epilepsy during early childhood and approximately 90 per cent develop their initial symptoms before age 20. Epileptic seizures vary considerably in their clinical manifestations. One feature common to most seizures is a sudden loss or impairment of consciousness. This may or may not be associated with convulsive movement or other abnormal or psychic performances. Tongue	After association with and observation of epileptics, some prediction or warning or seizures may be made. Patient should warn the teacher of an impending attack, if the warning is advanced enough, so preparation can be made. The warning is called an aura and takes the form of odd tastes, smells, noise, visual sensations, or abdominal or head pain. Most seizures can be controlled by medication, so teachers should be aware of the type of medicine used and see that the child is taking it. Seizures and their severity have been found to have relationships to allergy, alcohol, fluid intake, anesthetics,

scientifically defined the epilepsy as a "sudden, violent, disorderly discharge of the brain cells."

Many physicians classify epilepsies into two groups:

1. When the seizures occur following permanent brain changes or damage, it is called secondary, organic, or symptomatic epilepsy. Recurrent seizures which may follow brain injuries or infections of the brain such as menigitis and encephalitis, or disturbances of the brain which occur

biting, urinary incontinence, or fecal incontinence occurs in some patients, especially those with grand mall seizures. The three main classifications are as follows:

1. Grand mal. Patient loses consciousness, falls, and goes into rapid, generalized jerking movement. A loud cry may precede the onset. Breathing becomes labored and uneven; complexion may become flushed. These seizures may persist for 5 to 30 minutes. Patient may be exhausted and sleep following the seizure.

2. Petit mal. These are short seizures of from 5 to 10 seconds, rarely over 20 seconds. Patient

drugs, chemicals, and photic stimulation. Photic precipitation occurs through the patient observing a flickering light. This may be a defective overhead light or even a television set. Careful observation may allow the teacher to either interpret the cause of the seizure or to prevent it entirely. Schools should attempt to develop independence and self confidence in those children by doing some of the following:

1. Teach the child to protect himself according to the structional need. Anticipate the seizure and lie down, or don protective equipment. Putting objects in the mouth is not deemed necessary.

2. The teacher should provide daily physical exercise and teach the child its importance. The potential for seizures tends to lessen with good physical and mental exercise. Good general health should also be stressed.

Definition	*Manifestations*	*Educational Approaches or Techniques*
with lead intoxication, are examples of so-called secondary epilepsy. 2. When seizures occur in patients and the physician is unable to demonstrate specific evidence of a cerebral disturbance, the disorder is frequently labeled as idiopathic epilepsy. This condition is also known as cryptogenic (of obscure origin), essential, pure, primary, true, or genetic epilepsy.	usually appears pale and has vacant stare; may stumble, seldom falling. Usually no aftereffects. 3. Psychomotor seizure. It is characterized by automatic, stereotyped movement, or a variety of abnormal behavior manifestations associated with some clouding of consciousness and at least partial amnesia for the event. In young children, this may be characterized by an isolated automatism, such as smacking or chewing movements. There is evidence to believe that some persons can induce	3. Pressures of social situations have been known to bring on attacks, so the teacher needs to teach the child emotional discipline. 4. The child needs to participate and be successful in a variety of activities, not only to improve his self image but to give him a sense of the limits of his abilities. 5. At the same time, the child should learn to tolerate failure as well as success. This may require the teacher structuring controlled activity groups. 6. In a sense, the epileptic may need to be always dependent in a sense, so he must be taught depending as well as sharing. This may be taught through group planning, activities, and committee work, with the child playing controlling roles.

epileptic seizures at will. This would be a pseudoepileptic. This is a device used by individuals, which is thought to be similar to a temper tantrum.

7. Early vocational guidance should be taught so that realistic life goals are established. Teaching in modification of life styles may be necessary to avoid complications.

8. As the child becomes older, he should be taught the services available to him as a handicapped person, as well as any laws relative to his function as a normal person.

CEREBRAL PALSY

Definition

Cerebral palsy is a condition caused by damage to the human brain, usually at birth. It is estimated that there are 10,000 children with cerebral palsy born every year. These youngsters range in behavioral manifestations

Manifestations

Cerebral palsy may be described as a group of disabling conditions which will include impairment in any sense modality and intellectual impairment. Although not all children with cerebral palsy will have intellectual impairment, great caution should be

Educational Approaches or Techniques

There is no known treatment today that can promise a cure for cerebral palsy but those with the disease can have improvement throughout their lifetime. Every individual needs repeated diagnosis and treatment which may include braces, hearing aids, glasses, surgery, and physical and occupational therapy. Some suggestions for teachers are the following:

Definition

from imperceptible to gross motor problems. It is highly recommended that each child with cerebral palsy have a complete clinical examination. (Other disabilities found in the category will be discussed under separate titles, e.g. visual problems, hearing problems).

Manifestations

used in making intellectual judgement on such multiple-handicapped individuals. Cerebral palsy is characterized by paralysis, weakness, incoordination, or any other abnormality of motor function.

Various forms of the disorder are classified into three main types:

a. Spastic, where individual moves stiffly and with difficulty.

b. Athetoid, where individual has involuntary and uncontrolled movements.

c. Ataxia, where sense of balance and depth perception are disturbed.

Educational Approaches or Techniques

1. Psycho-social

a. Involve student with total program at every opportunity, full participation (e.g. if he cannot shoot baskets, at least have him keep score).

b. Overprotection should be avoided; encourage him in everything.

c. Remember this student is hurt more by lack of participation than by a bruised knee; however, care should be taken that failure does not lead to lower self-esteem.

d. Strengths should be emphasized (e.g. if he is the best checker player, opportunity should be given to emphasize importance).

2. Neuro-muscular training.

a. Physical education program should be one in which the student is given the opportunity to use his motor skills.
   1) Tumbling.
   2) Trampoline.
   3) Games.
   4) Wrestling.
   5) Floor movements, such as creeping, crawling.
   6) Swimming.

b. Classroom program.
   1) Music, such marching, hopping, skipping, etc.
   2) Glider, walkers.
   3) Tricycle.
   4) Jungle gym.
   5) Blocks, puzzles.
   6) Dumbbells, Indian clubs.
   7) Training stairs.

c. A teacher may need to assist the student to adjust to daily living skills.
   1) Toilet training, buttoning.

Definition	Manifestations	Educational Approaches or Techniques
		2) Feeding—swallowing, chewing, blowing.
		3) Breathing-controlled breath.
		4) Bracing—knowledge of orthopedic procedures for proper bracing support.
		5) Knowledge of special fields can be obtained by specialized reading.
		a) Occupational therapy.
		b) Physical therapy.
		c) Speech therapy.
		d) Parent counseling in groups and by organizations that give social, spiritual, and educational help (e.g. Summer Easter Seal Camps).

LOW VITALITY

Definition

The student who lacks the physical stamina for a full day of school activity is one with low vitality. This condition is of a consistent nature and has become a regular behavioral pattern exhibited by the student.

Manifestations

The manifestations shown in this condition by the student are

1. Consistent drowziness.
2. Consistent lack of enthusiasm.
3. Consistently slow body movements.
4. Consistent lack of facial and body expression.
5. Consistent pale and shallow facial coloring.

Educational Approaches or Techniques

The teacher must consider a number of factors that contribute to this condition; the physical as well as the psychological factor, or a combination of these. Broken down, the factors might be as follows:

1. Physical.
   a. Lack of rest—improper sleep habits.
   b. Poor nutrition—lack of proper diet.
   c. Body abuse—smoking, drugs, glue sniffing, alcohol, etc.
   d. Physical complications—anemia, diabetes, hypothyroidism, etc.
2. Psychological.
   a. Serious emotional problems.
   b. Transient anxiety—family problems, peer adjustment, etc.

Definition

Manifestations

Educational Approaches or Techniques

    c. Poor self-concept—inferior feelings interfere with his ability to concentrate on work because of energy used to combat inferior feelings toward self.

Following are some suggestions for teachers:

1. Complete medical examination recommended to parents and followed through with the school nurse.
2. Parent counseling. Home visit would be the best. Management of the home is most important to understand. food habits, sleeping habits, general health habits, etc. Recommendations should be made as needs are recognized.
3. School adjustments.
    a. Nutritional aid to younger children in poor socioeconomic

levels. Work out a nutritional program with school board and school cafeteria personnel. State and federal funds may be available to supplement nutritional habits of your student. Breakfast and snack periods have been provided in certain schools throughout the country.

b. Rest. For younger children, provide rest periods throughout the day. A child who is fatigued can only accomplish what is asked for in school when he has had the proper amount of rest.

c. Teaching aids. The teacher should provide, when need is felt, *unit*-presentations on health. These units should concentrate on nutrition, rest, drugs, smoking, and other important factors that have a

Definition

Manifestations

Educational Approaches or Techniques

bearing on the health of your students. The use of outside resources are a must in providing such a program (e.g. field trips, resource personnel, health pamphlets, etc.).

d. Ego-development. The teacher should, when the student lacks good ego-strengths, be an ego-builder. Provide success situations for students that give them a better feeling about themselves. This type of student can only achieve in school when he feels good about himself. The teacher needs to make a consistent effort in providing rewarding situations for such students.

DIABETIC CHILD

Definition

Diabetes occurs when the pancreas is unable to produce insulin. Deficient insulin creates a problem in the body's ability to use food substances, particularly sugar. An abnormal concentration of sugar occurs in the blood and urine. Fats, which depend upon the presence of sugar for their effective conversion into usable forms, are not adequately utilized.

Manifestations

Diabetes is particularly severe during childhood, since the demand of the growing body is great and most activity is at a high rate. As a rule, diabetic children appear healthy and well at first. An important symptom is persisting fatigue, which is due to the unavailability of sugars and the secondary inability to use fats. Hunger becomes important as a symptom, since foods are not properly converted into usable nutritive substances. Other symptoms usually include excessive thirst, excessive urination, loss of weight, slow healing of cuts and bruises, changes in vision, in-

Educational Approaches or Techniques

Because diabetes can be critical to the longevity of the child, careful considerations should be made for classroom maintainence.

1. Children's reactions to diabetes show great variation in behavior and personality characteristics. Usually, however, they are frightened children because their mode of life is different. The teacher should attempt to alleviate these fears by acceptance and guidance.

2. Parental reactions to the diabetic child are likely to be either of two: oversolicitous coddling or resentment and rejection. The teacher may thus have to modify attitudes of peers and himself because the child's reaction to his

Definition	Manifestations	Educational Approaches or Techniques
	tense itching, pain in fingers and toes, and drowsiness.	ailment will depend to a marked degree on how he is treated by significant others.
	Children who have diabetes react to various life situations as though they were deprived of food. Their adaptive reactions are appropriate to conditions of starvation. Emotional stress is often a precipitating factor in the onset of diabetes.	3. The teacher should be aware that when a diabetic child appears listless, inattentive, restless, or irritable, he is not to be accused of being lazy but may need a new balance in his medical therapy. Once this is established, a child can participate in normal activities.
		4. The teacher should be aware of the consequences if the child fails to eat promptly, neglects his insulin, or overexercises. He may go into insulin shock, becoming dizzy and light-headed, suffer abdominal pain, or other symptoms. A piece of candy, lump of sugar, or glass of orange juice will often quickly restore him to normal.

5. Should a coma occur, prompt medical attention is recommended.

6. Once a medical program has been worked out with periodic check-ups to maintain a good insulin-sugar balance, the diabetic child should be treated as any other child and does not need special class placement or other special considerations.

APHASIA

Symbolization defects are manifest to some degree in internal symbol processes (thinking), as well as external symbol processes (speaking, reading, writing).

Severe aphasic children should be referred to experts for educational purposes, or the educators should read extensively in the literature before approaching the educational task. Expert diagnostic studies are helpful.

Educational processes have taken several directions. One method which has proven most successful is learning through

Aphasic disturbances are impairments in the ability of the individual to behave appropriately in situations which involve a significant amount of symbolization. Often the classifications of aphasia are referred to as receptive (patient's ability in

Definition	*Manifestations*	*Educational Approaches or Techniques*
the comprehension of spoken and written symbols) or expressive (patient's ability to express ideas in speech and/or in writing).		writing. 1. Careful presentation and learning of a few sounds of letters and of certain combinations of letters at one time through the associative process of hearing, seeing, sounding, and writing the symbol of these sounds is an accepted approach. 2. Writing is one of the links in the chain of communication that shows the greatest impairment. Training is done through painstaking and slow repetition of letters, then words, then sentences. 3. Speech is trained along with reading and writing by saying and seeing and, if necessary, getting the student to feel the way sounds are made. 4. Problems in children with deficit visiospatial component experiences in recognizing letters, words, and the engrams of speech may also cause

great distress in learning arithmetic. Very concrete material should be used that can be held, moved, and counted. Avoid teaching varied "patterns of arithmetic."

5. Aphasic children are usually not outgoing and have disorientation to time and space. They must be trained for independence through graded help. They should be encouraged to mix and join in normal social activities.

HARD OF HEARING

A person labeled hard of hearing is one who has a recorded loss on audiometric examination of from 16 to 82 decibels. Hearing is functional for language purposes with limitations, with or without a hearing aid.

The hard of hearing student manifests a wide variety of characteristics that finds these students exhibiting superior to poor school achievement. There are a wide number of variables that may contribute to either their success or failure in school. The most common in school. The most common in school. The most common ure in school. The most com-

The regular classroom teacher, if special classes or itinerant teachers are not available, should do the following:

1. Have adequate hearing examinations and up-to-date records on each student along with some interpretation as to the nature of the hearing loss.

2. When speaking to the student,

Definition	Manifestations	Educational Approaches or Techniques
	mon denominator for success or failure is the effort and concern of parents and teachers, and the provisions of special educational programs. Hard of hearing students face many frustrating and emotion-laden situations because of their hearing loss. These problems and concerns are often overlooked because of the students' normal appearance and their ability to make normal social adjustments, despite the fact they have not correctly aurally appraised the situation, nor grasped the abstract nature of the concept presented. Hearing problems often create abnormal anxiety reactions as well as frustrations and can lead to social isolation.	have his direct visual attention. 3. If the student does not understand the first time, instead of raising the voice, restate the idea, using a different language approach. 4. Encourage group academic and social intercourse with normal-hearing children. 5. When counseling parents, encourage them to involve the child in community group activities. 6. Most children with extremes of hearing loss have some speech problems. Refer the child to a speech therapist. 7. Check on the students' hearing aid needs, including use, care, and regular check-ups. 8. Encourage the student to challenge himself and to recognize that he is handicapped but not disabled. Frequent positive reinforcement will assist in his

This disability is described as referring to persons in whom the sense of hearing is nonfunctional for the ordinary language requirements of life. The hearing loss is recorded on an audiometer as 82 decibels or greater. The degree to which deafness affects school achievement and school participation is determined by (a) age of onset, (b) intelligence, and (c) type of loss. It must be remembered that total deafness is con-

motivation.

9. Further information is given under the "Deafness" title.

DEAFNESS

It has been found that deaf children are almost universally below average in school achievement. Their competency has been found to be directly related to their ability to understand and use language, especially in the areas of abstractions and their comprehension. The social competency of deaf children has been found to be below that of children their own age. The hearing disability does not allow the child to be exposed to the developmental social skills of normal-hearing children, and as a consequence,

Appropriately, the teacher of deaf children should have specialized training. However, until the teacher receive training, the following few suggestions may prove helpful:

1. The teacher should obtain a certified and adequate record of the students' hearing capabilities.

2. The teacher should recommend adequate placement of such a student in a special classroom for deaf children. If this is not possible, an itinerant teacher who could help the student on a regular basis and also give instruction to the regular teacher would be advised. The types of programs recommended might include:

Definition	Manifestations	Educational Approaches or Techniques
sidered the most total life incapacitating disability.	social skills of deaf children are primitive and in some cases bizarre.	a. Multi-sensory training, b. speech reading, c. use of a hearing aid (if necessary), d. emphasize social participation, e. work on self-concept, f. family counseling. 3. The regular class teacher should work closely with the itinerant teacher or special regular classroom teacher on adjustments. Such methods include: a. Individual counseling, b. encouraging social participation with peer hearing children, c. speaking clearly with correct pronunciation and enunciation, d. facing the light so lips are observable, e. encouraging classroom speech, f. using multi-sensory approaches with multi-media of the same

concept,

g. using natural speech,

h. never using speech without voice.

Quantity of speech is thought to be more important than quality of speech during the educational stages.

TACTILE DISABILITY

This is an insensitivity to discriminate different sensations of feeling through skin contact (disability in tactile discrimination level).

This disability is present within the student who is insensitive to

1. Pain. Student may be continually injured but does not respond appropriately.
2. Textural configuration. Student is unable to tell the difference between the surfaces of objects.
3. Thermal sensations. Student is unaware of temperature.

If learning can take place through other intact senses, then the tactile or haptic sensory approach to learning may be circumvented. Multisensory teaching may only confuse some students. If, however, the sense needs developing to avoid injury or because it is undeveloped, then some of the following may be used:

1. Blind symbol tracing. Trace symbols or numbers as the child is blindfolded.
2. Fernald method. Trace patterns with fingers, using various tex-

Definition	Manifestations	Educational Approaches or Techniques
	4. Kinesthetic sensations. Student has inability to discriminate between articles of different weights, or of direction or force of things or self in motion, as a child who loses his balance easily when turning rapidly in play activity.	tures, such as sandpaper and clay, or in the air.
		3. Object identification. Objects placed in a bag or hidden from sight and the student identifies the objects by feel alone.
		4. Tactile surfaces. Teacher prepares different tactile surfaces that the child may feel (e.g. various grades of texture or finish).
		5. Liquid discrimination of different water temperatures and viscosities.
		6. Teaching the children situations which may avoid painful injuries.
		7. Brushing. Stroke various areas of the child's skin with various pressures and textures.
		Material by the following persons may be used as resources and references: Fernald, Montessori, Kephart, and Ayers.

GROSS MOTOR IMPAIRMENT

Definition

Gross motor impairment is best described as awkward and clumsy motor function or body movement. A student who has this disability, when performing tasks involving gross motor activities, appears uncoordinated; and his performance is below expectations for the child's chronological age.

Manifestations

This student has difficulty participating competitively with his peers in sports and games. Also, he may often be having difficulty in academic areas (i.e. subject matter, reading), classroom management, and classroom movement. He may run into desks and other objects and in general have problems navigating stairs, playground equipment, and other obstacles to free movement. These difficulties do not appear to be related to vision. Inability to perform fine-discrimination manual tasks is the most obvious observable indicator. Many of these children are physically de-

Educational Approaches or Techniques

The educational literature is replete with suggestions that success in skill subjects is somehow related to body coordination and that children showing good academic ability are usually well coordinated, agile, quick, and do not exhibit awkward or clumsy behavior. Recently focus has been directed to the retraining of children through early primitive creep, crawl, and cross-patterning exercises to correct learning problems. Empirical evidence is not available to prove this can cure academic problems, but, as has already been suggested, any exercise which involves the student in complete body movement should be a regular part of his daily educational program. If a teacher has a child with a coordination problem in his class, there should be a

Definition	Manifestations	Educational Approaches or Techniques
	scribed as "big for their age," "grew too fast," "all hands and feet," or receive other names such as "clumsy," "awkward," or even "stupid."	portion of each day set aside for such training. This type of program could be written out on an individual basis and given to the student so that he could "self-tutor" his own program. The recommendations for the exercises for such a program are as follows: 1. Running in place (standing still and running up and down). 2. Skipping rope (if the child is old enough). This will take time but is excellent for developing coordination. 3. One-legged jumps (stand on one leg, jump, and then change legs and jump again). 4. Tumbling—"front roll" (student starts with his hands on the mat, feet back, and turns himself over). Doing these in a consistent one-after-another manner is recommended.

5. Jumping jacks.

6. Space movement (student makes fast movement to left, right, backwards, forwards, as quickly as possible).

7. Walking board or line (student must maintain equilibrium as he moves along straight line).

8. Angels in the snow (moving arms and legs, on command, from a prone position, lying on front or back).

9. Crawling through limited spaces, such as barrels or tubes.

10. Decathlon race, which requires a change in motor activity over an obstacle course, which requires running, walking, crawling, skipping, etc.

The above examples are only a few of the many different types of coordination drills which can be given to students with gross motor problems. What should be kept in mind is that

Definition	Manifestations	Educational Approaches or Techniques
		such a program can be devised very easily and implemented into the student's program. Activities should progress from gross motor to fine motor and from simple to complex.

IV

MENTAL HEALTH IN THE CLASSROOM

GOOD mental health is the absence of poor mental health. This may be as appropriate an explanation of good mental health as can be made when dealing with a subject as complicated as the human mind. However, in visiting many classrooms, we have found that it is not difficult to discern that there are factors at work between teacher and student which seem to produce a learning atmosphere in which children become eager, enthusiastic, contented learners or become anxious, malcontent, disruptive agitators. Recent research by the United States Department of Health, Education and Welfare reveals that the dropout rate has a close correlation to the mental health of students. It is true that children bring many of their problems from the home environment, yet it is not impossible to find teachers who can take children who come from disturbed backgrounds and integrate them into classrooms until it is difficult to tell them from nondisturbed children. It is more than a teacher with an emotionally stable, mature personality that makes the difference. It is the ability of this teacher to create a total school atmosphere or milieu conducive to good mental health and learning. It is the total milieu factors which we will attempt to spell out here.

A primary technique for a teacher to practice would be total acceptance. This means the acceptance of all children on the basis of what they are rather than what the teacher would like them to be. When teachers are overheard talking about students as dirty, poor, ugly, or other negative phrases, it can be believed that these teachers have failed to see the beauty and unexploited potential of children.

Good expectations is another positive valence factor influencing the success or failure of a student. A teacher who has set high expectations in behavior, as well as academic success, can only fall short of the goal, while teachers who have low expectations and negative feelings and goals may easily reach their expectancy levels. Research points out the fact that behavioral levels rise with the level of the teachers' expectations. If poor behavior and low expectation levels are anticipated, they will be fulfilled quickly and detrimentally to both the teacher and the student.

A two-way communication system is necessary in order for a teacher to understand the students' feelings. All messages should be clear and specific. Good teaching can only be established by listening to the expressed needs of the child. Stop telling him what to do all the time because, after listening, it may be discovered that he has a reasonable explanation for his behavior. Because we think in verbal mediators, it is best, when possible, to have a child express himself in verbal communication. This is especially important if a teacher is to discipline a child; before the child is disciplined, he should formulate in words the reason for the penalty.

Children need to be surrounded by a world which is predictable. If one does a particular act, the environment reponds with a certain reaction. These reactions may be positive or negative, depending on the act. If a child does well and the teacher reinforces the act with positive encouragement, it is highly possible that the child will continue this type of action. The opposite is also true, and negative behavior can be reinforced in some rather bizarre ways. An extreme case would be a child whose only attention at home or school is through punishment. He becomes so mentally sick that he learns to receive attention by creating a disturbance to the point of being punished. This type of world is predictable but negatively so. It is expected that the world created for the child will be one of positive prediction with techniques used for handling negative behavior other than those of physical punishment. Deprivation of a privilege, as well as isolation, are more acceptable than the adverse control of physical beatings.

Consistency enters the picture here and may be associated with a predictable world in order that there must be consistency in order. In addition, however, there is the need for all persons coming in contact with the child to treat him the same. Another aspect is that the teacher maintains consistent mood tones from day to day in his exposure to the child. Excessive mood swings by a teacher are evidence of poor mental health.

Children need good ego models on which to pattern behavior. No teacher should ever have to tell a student, "Don't do as I do, do as I say." Psychologists are always amazed to find children with poor behaviors they have learned from teachers. The younger a child is, the greater the imitative ability. Again, the best teacher would be one who is free of emotional hang-ups, poor health habits, and even poor speech or personal mannerisms.

An atmosphere of approval and positive reinforcement should be fostered. A teacher can create this by positively reinforcing good behavior while ignoring minor misbehavior. Poor behavior, not reinforced, will often become extinct. Classrooms should be filled with child-made papers and art work. Instead of writing failing grades on papers, let the child do them over until they are acceptable for posting. Nothing is gained for a child's self-concept by negative reinforcement and the giving of poor grades for school work. A child can learn to hate schools and teachers if he receives enough frustrations through failures. There are few children who are not affected by disapproval through grades or verbal assaults.

Classrooms should be child learning centers. The room is the child's stage for performance. The teacher sits in the background as a director of activities. Nothing in the room should be teacher-created. All work or projects in the room should originate from the children. The room should be "our room" and "we do things" rather than "Mrs. Smith's room." It should be remembered that if a child has an invested interest in the room, he will defend it.

Special consideration should be given to children who come to school emotionally ill. This may require a therapy conference with the child before school starts. Teachers should be in their rooms and objectively aware of the students as they enter in the morning to see the temperament of each individual. An understanding comment should be made to try to dissolve some of the anxieties children bring from home. Some children benefit from being touched during the day. This means that when a teacher knows a child is in trouble, he should place a friendly, accepting hand on the child's shoulder as he moves past him. Verbal comments need not be made.

There is no substitute for well-prepared, interesting lessons. Proper preparations, with lessons geared to children's abilities, will create an atmosphere of interest and absorption in the learning situation rather than attempts to seek satisfactions from manipulating the environment through misbehavior. Children who find only frustration and failure in academic tasks soon learn to avoid them and usually turn to causing distractions in the classroom.

Teachers often ask how a class can gain intrinsic controls or behavior controls coming from within the children rather than from extrinsic or imposed controls. Careful observation reveals that this will occur where a teacher is a warm, accepting, emotionally mature individual, where the teacher has good two-way communication, where the teacher uses positive reinforcement and frequent praise, where the teacher is a director of education and leaves some of the program development to students, where the teacher is willing to give himself away with concern and love, where the teacher sees the continued wonderment of life unfolding in the young, where the teacher is spontaneous and accepts his own self-humanness of making. mistakes, where the teacher assumes the responsibilities of professional obligations to prepare lessons geared to the prescribed needs of children, and where the teacher is not limited by today but dreams of future realities. There is not much more our educational system can offer.

V

BEHAVIOR MODIFICATION

A GREAT deal of interest has been generated in recent years concerning the conditioning of behavior, by appropriate methods so that the individual will respond in a manner established by the teacher. Courses covering these methods are now taught in colleges, and complete programmed material may be purchased for self-teaching. Holland and Skinner have published a book of this nature entitled *The Analysis of Behavior,* (McGraw-Hill, 1961), or use G. J. Bensberg's *Teaching The Mentally Retarded: A Handbook For Ward Personnel* (Atlanta, 1965).

The following presentation of operant conditioning is only meant to be a brief description of this particular method. If the teacher desires to learn more, the above-recommended literature would be a helpful start. The operant conditioning method is primarily concerned with developing meaningful, self-directive behavior in people. The behavior desired is of such a nature that it may come under the individual's control. It is the teacher's responsibility to first define the behavior she desires the individual to accomplish. Once the teacher has defined such behavior, she then may apply the second principle of operant conditioning, that of reinforcement. The term "reinforcement" refers to the rewarding of a person for exhibiting the desired behavior as previously defined by the teacher. Such reinforcements as money, attention, food, or special activities may be provided by the teacher. So the method basically consists of defining desired behavior to be exhibited by the student and reinforcing the behavior when it is actually displayed by the student. In using this method, the teacher assumes that learning occurs because the person receives some form of reinforcement for doing the desired act.

It is vital in using this method that the teacher become a keen observer and recorder of behaviors. The teacher who is able to

97

describe in behavioral terms the types of behavior that she desires in her classroom will have a greater chance of success in applying this approach. It is not enough to state that we want our student to be a "better boy." The teacher must describe what behaviors she expects of this student if he is to reach this goal. It must be clear to the teacher what the "good" represents in action.

Another key to success in using operant conditioning is finding and using appropriate reinforcers. It is true that not all students react in a positive way to the same type of reinforcement. To borrow from the "times," somethings turn some people on, whereas they do nothing for others. The teacher must be aware of this fact and use reinforcers that are motivating for the student and turn him on to action in the appropriate behavioral pattern. Also, students react at different times in different ways to reinforcers, again demanding flexibility in this area by the teacher.

It is recommended that the teacher ask the student what his particular preference for reinforcement is and use this particular one until the student needs a change. It is important that the teacher be flexible and willing to police and change these reinforcers. The success of the program depends on the motivation generated by such reinforcers.

In summary, an operant conditioning program can be started by any teacher working with any student, the requirement being that the teacher is a student of behavior and can define such behavioral action so that she can judge its appropriateness or inappropriateness in any situation and that the teacher understands the different types of reinforcers that can be applied to strengthen the occurrence of desired behavior by the student.

VI

BIBLIOGRAPHY

Bateman, B.: Learning disabilities. In Frierson, C. E. and Barbe, W. B. (Eds.): Educating Children with Learning Disabilities. New York: Appleton-Century-Crofts, 1967, pp. 19-22.

Bryant, Dale: Characteristics of dyslexia and their remedial implication. Exceptional Children, 31:195-199, December, 1965.

Clements, S. D., and Peters, J. E.: Minimal brain dysfunction in the school-age child. In Frierson, C. E. and Barbe, W. B. (Eds.): Educating Children with Learning Disabilities. New York: Appleton-Century-Crofts, 1967, pp. 66-84.

Crothers, Bronson and Paine, Richmond S.: The Natural History of Cerebral Palsy. Cambridge, Harvard University Press, 1959.

Cruickshank, William M.: The Brain-Injured Child in Home, School and Community. Syracuse: Syracuse University, 1967, pp. 27-66 and 156-157.

Dupont, Henry: Educating Emotionally Disturbed Children. New York: Holt, Rinehart and Winston, 1969.

Egg, Maria: When A Child is Different. New York: John Day, 1964.

Ellingson, Careth: The Shadow Children. Chicago: Topan Books, 1967.

Fletcher, H. L.: Suggestions on correcting left to right reversals in reading and writing. In Teaching Educationally Handicapped Children. San Rafael, Calif.: Academic Therapy Publication, 1967, pp. 41-45.

Gigous, G. M.: Improving Listening Skills. Dansville, New York: F. A. Owen, 1967, pp. 6-48.

Goldberg, Maxwell H.: Blindness Research: The Expanding Frontiers. University Park: Pennsylvania State University Press, 1969.

Haring, Norris G. and Phillips, Lakin E.: Educating Emotionally Disturbed Children. New York: McGraw-Hill, 1962.

Hathaway, Winifred: Education and Health of the Partially Seeing Child. New York: Columbia University Press, 1959.

Jones, John Walker and Collins, Anne P.: Educational Programs for Visually Handicapped Children. Washington: U.S. Government Printing Office, 1966.

Kaliski, L.: Arithmetic and the Brain-Injured Child. In Frierson, C. E. and Barbe, W. B. (Eds.): Educating Children with Learning Disabilities. New

York: Appleton-Century-Crofts, 1967.

Knights, R. M. and Thompson, A. A.: Training Suggestions for Children with Specific Learning Deficits. Research Bulletin No. 12. Ontario, Canada: University of Western Ontario, September, 1966.

Lewis, R. S., Strauss, A. A. and Lehtinen, L. E.: The Other Child. New York: Grune and Stratton, 1960.

Levine, N. and Carter, C.: Handwriting for the Learning-Disabled. Academic Therapy Quarterly. Vol. IV, no. 1, Fall, 1968.

Lukoff, Irving and Whiteman, Martin: The Social Sources of Adjustment to Blindness. Montpelier, Vt.: Capital City Press,

McCarthy, J. McRae: How to teach the hard-to-reach. Reprint Grade Teacher, May/June, 1967.

McLeod, J.: Some perceptual factors related to childhood dyslexia. The Slow Learning Child. Vol. 14, no. 1, July, 1967.

Myklebust, Helmer R.: Your Deaf Child. Springfield: Thomas, 1950.

Myklebust, Helmer R. and Boshes, B.: Psychoneurological learning disorders in children. In Frierson, C. E. and Barbe, W. B. (Eds.): Educating Children with Learning Disabilities. New York: Appleton-Century-Crofts, 1967.

Nitchie, Elizabeth Helm: New Lessons in Lip Reading. Philadelphia: J. B. Lippincott, 1950.

Proceedings of the Forty-Ninth Biennial Conference, Association For Education of the Visually Handicapped. Toronto, Canada, 1968.

Rainer, John D. and Altshuler, Kenneth Z.: Psychiatry and the Deaf. Washington: U. S. Depatment of Health, Education, and Welfare, 1967.

Rowe, C. A.: Techniques for teaching dyslexic children. Academic Therapy Quarterly, Vol. III, no. 3, Spring, 1968.

Serio, M. and Faelchle, J.: No giant steps please: A visual and auditory approach to reading. Academic Therapy Quarterly, Vol. III, no. 3, Spring, 1968.

Shields, O. L.: Remediation of learning disabilities in a public school system. Mental Retardation, December, 1965.

Signor, Roger: Hyperactive children. (A study by Mark A. Stewart, Assistant Professor of Pediatrics and Psychiatry.) Washington University Magazine. Vol. 37, no. 2. Winter, 1967.

Silver, Archie, A.: Diagnostic considerations in children with reading disability. Reprinted from Bulletin of the Orton Society, Vol. XI, May, 1961.

Teaching Brain-Injured Children. Curriculum Bulletin, 1966-67. Series No. 12. Brooklyn: Board of Education of the City of New York, 1967.

Valett, Robert: The Remediation of Learning Disabilities. A Handbook of Psychoeducational Resource Programs. "Perceptual — Motor Skills," "Language Development" and "Conceptual Skills." Palo Alto, Calif.: Fearson, 1967.

VII

INSTRUCTIONAL MATERIALS

DEFINITION OF TERMS

THIS section contains a list of instructional materials. These materials are now being produced for use with exceptional children in classrooms around the country. Many of these items are designed for children with specific disabilities, while others can be used with any child to enhance his learning process. The materials recorded here are found in the Instructional Material Center at Bowling Green State University and are available for examination and use by teachers working in the university's geographic areas. The materials found in this center are typical of those found in other facilities throughout the United States. These are available on a library-loan basis without charge.

In order to make the materials as meaningful as possible, each was examined and categorized on the charts. Because of the small spaces for categorization, it was not possible to amplify descriptions or interpret terms. Additional interpretation will be made at this point. Explanation will be made of the column headings from left to right.

Company. A list of the complete addresses of each company can be found in the bibliography.

Item. In some cases, the item may be records, film, filmstrips, books, games, etc. Wherever necessary, this is explained under "other comments."

Author. In some cases, materials are credited to companies and offer no author. In these instances, the author space is left blank.

Other Comments. An effort was made here to describe whether the material was a book, filmstrip, etc. In some cases, the examiners have added additional remarks about the construction or composition of the items.

Child. The EMR refers to the educable mentally retarded, which is the kind of child found in the larger majority of special school classes. Separation of these children is usually done on the basis of standardized individual I.Q. tests. Scores for EMR range from 50 to 80 I.Q. The causes of retardation may vary from hereditary or genetic to injury, psychological causes, social causes, or disease entities. No effort is made here to differentiate cause of retardation.

The TMR refers to the trainable mentally retarded, with the individual scores of below 50 I.Q. This group is thought to be unable to benefit from formal academic training. Most training is directed towards habit or social education. The cerebral palsy classification is thought to be self-explanatory as well as the physically or orthopedically handicapped. The blind refers to individuals who test on the Snellen Chart above 20/200. Partially sighted refers to the visually-impaired child testing 20/70 to 20/200, as measured by the Snellen Chart. The gifted are those children with superior I.Q.'s, or they are referred to by some as gifted if they have a talent or special ability.

Age Groups. Further division of children could be made by age or grade, but because most of these materials are for special classes, divisions were made into the four categories of special classes: primary, intermediate, junior high, and senior high.

Cost. This was found to be a highly subjective evaluation on the part of the examiners, in most cases. Determination of hierarchy cost was partially made on the basis of the quality and quantity of the material in relation to price. In some cases, the actual price is given and the decision left to the individual purchaser.

Applicable For. All material was carefully examined by an

experienced special education teacher and judgement was made as to the intended application, based on the material itself as well as on the author's intentions for the material.

Clear Instruction. An effort was made to judge the clarity and preciseness of the instructions accompanying the material. It was found that some materials required some sophistication and background in educational techniques as well as certain philosophies and rationales of certain medical, psychological, or social disciplines before accurate interpretations could be made.

Company	Item	Publisher or Author	Comments
Paul. S. Amidon and Associates	Mark-Away Program	Marian F. Calway	Teacher guide-sheets, card, plastic sheet, marking pencil
	Set RA Unit 1		
	Unit 1 Set 1A		
	Unit 1 Set 3A		
	Unit 1 Set 1D		
	Unit 2 Set 2B		
	Unit 1 Set 3B		
Ann Arbor Publishers	Michigan Language Program	Donald P. Smith and Judith M. Smith	
	A Program for Teachers		
	D1 Writing Words		Child's workbook
	Visual Tracking		Self-instruction workbook
	B Writing Letters		Teachers manual
	Book D		
	Listening 2 Reading Letters		Teachers manual
American Educational Publication (AEP)	Phonics & Word Power		Phonetics
	Program 1		Practice book
	Program 2		Practice book
	Program 3		Practice book

Educable Retarded	Trainable Retarded	Cerebral Palsy Victim	Physically Handicapped	Partially Sighted	Blind	Hard-of-Hearing	Gifted	Primary	Intermediate	Junior High	Senior High	Free	Low	Medium	High	Make-It-Yourself	Visual Perception	Auditory Perception	Eye-Hand Coordination	Fine Finger Coordination	Gross Motor	Poor Sequencing	Other	Yes	No	Reading
x	x							x	x				x			x	x	x	x					x		
x	x							x	x				x			x	x	x	x					x		
x	x							x	x				x			x	x	x	x					x		
x	x							x	x				x			x	x	x	x					x		
x	x							x	x				x			x	x	x	x					x		
x	x							x	x				x			x	x	x	x					x		
	x							x	x								x							x		
	x							x	x															x		
	x							x	x								x							x		
	x							x	x								x							x		
	x							x	x								x							x		
x								x	x			x											x	x		x
x								x	x			x											x	x		x
x								x	x			x											x	x		x

Company	Item	Publisher or Author	Comments
AEP	New Science Reading Adventures		Science concepts vocabulary; grade levels 1-6; Practice books
AEP	Read, Study, Think		Grades 2-6
AEP	Reading Success		Reading
AEP	Map Skills Today		Second-grade reading level
AEP	Table and Graph Skills		Third-grade reading level
AEP	Imagine and Write		Third-sixth grade levels
AEP	Science Unit Books		20 titles
AEP	Know Your World		Weekly paper
AEP	You and Your World		Weekly paper
AEP	Read		Pamphlet
AEP	Current Events		Social studies
AEP	Everyweek		Social studies
AEP	Our Times		U.S. history
AEP	Current Science		Science
AEP	Urban World		News
AEP	Paperback club		Novels, Paperbacks
AEP	ZIP'S Books		Science language skills
AEP	Buddy's Book of Puzzles		Reading skills

Educable Retarded	Trainable Retarded	Cerebral Palsy Victim	Physically Handicapped	Partially Sighted	Blind	Hard-of-Hearing	Gifted	Primary	Intermediate	Junior High	Senior High	Free	Low	Medium	High	Make-It-Yourself	Visual Perception	Auditory Perception	Eye-Hand Coordination	Fine Finger Coordination	Gross Motor	Poor Sequencing	Other	Yes	No	Reading
								x	x				x										x	x	x	
								x	x				x										x	x	x	
								x	x				x										x	x	x	
x										x			x										x	x	x	
										x			x										x	x	x	
										x			x										x	x	x	
										x			x										x	x	x	
x										x			x										x	x		
x											x		x										x	x		
										x			x										x	x		
										x			x										x	x		
					x						x												x	x		
					x						x		x										x	x		
					x					x			x										x	x		
					x					x	x		x										x	x		
					x					x	x		x										x	x		
x								x									x	x				x	x	x		
x								x									x						x	x		

Company	Item	Publisher or Author	Comments
Addison-Wesley	Elementary school English		Series of textbooks; not designed for special students; gifted could use.
Alda Instruments Ltd.	AAATA System		Multiple-answering teaching aid; provides instant reinforcement, feedback, and evaluation
Acousta	Wireless auditory trainer		
Aim Industries	Tabletamer		Circuit boards for math concepts; instant reward or correction
Aim Industries	Fractionfinder		
Aim Industries	Circuit Board		
Aim Industries	Speak-Easy		Recorder-Player
Allen	Teenagers Prepare for Work	Easter O. Carson	Work texts
	Campus Work Experience	Esther O. Carson	Work texts
Allied Educational Council	Book 1301; The Mott Basic Language Skills Program		Workbooks Book 1: Reading Skills
	Book 1302		Workbook 2: Reading Skills
	Book 1303		Workbook 3: Reading Skills
	Book 1304		Workbook 4: Reading Skills
	Book 1305		Workbook 5: Reading Skills
	Book 1306		Workbook 6: Reading Skills
	Book 1307		Workbook 7: Reading Skills

	Educable Retarded	Trainable Retarded	Cerebral Palsy Victim	Physically Handicapped	Partially Sighted	Blind	Hard-of-Hearing	Gifted	Primary	Intermediate	Junior High	Senior High	Free	Low	Medium	High	Make-It-Yourself	Visual Perception	Auditory Perception	Eye-Hand Coordination	Fine Finger Coordination	Gross Motor	Poor Sequencing	Other	Yes	No
Child →																										
								x	x	x							x								x	
	x	x		x	x				x	x	x	x					x							x	x	
					x	x			x	x	x						x							x	x	
	x											x					x							x	x	
	x											x					x							x	x	
								x									x								x	
																								x		
	x										x	x			x										x	x
	x										x	x			x										x	x
	x									x	x														x	x
	x									x	x														x	x
	x									x	x														x	x
	x										x														x	x
	x										x														x	x
	x											x													x	x

Other column, rows 2–7: "Language development reading"

Company	Item	Publisher or Author	Comments
	Book 1308		Workbook 8: Reading Skills
	Book 1309		Workbook 9: Reading Skills
	Book 1310		Workbook 10: Reading Skills
	Book 1505		Teacher materials
	Book 2001, Sound and Structure		Workbook
	Book 2002, Manual		Instruction manual
	Book 2003, Comprehension Series		Workbook
	Book 2004, Comprehension Series		Workbook
	Book 2005, Comprehension Series		Workbook
	Book 2006, Comprehension Series		Workbook
Alpay 3M Company	Alphy's Show & Tell		Basic reading series
American Art Class Company	Craft clays		Art supplies
American Art Class Company	Art materials		Art supplies
American Art Class Company	Chalk, white and colored		Art supplies
American Art Class Company	Craft supplies		Art supplies

Educable Retarded	Trainable Retarded	Cerebral Palsy Victim	Physically Handicapped	Partially Sighted	Blind	Hard-of-Hearing	Gifted	Primary	Intermediate	Junior High	Senior High	Free	Low	Medium	High	Make-It-Yourself	Visual Perception	Auditory Perception	Eye-Hand Coordination	Fine Finger Coordination	Gross Motor	Poor Sequencing	Other	Language development reading	Yes	No
																								Child → *Age Group* → *Cost* → *Applicable for Pupils with These Learning Disabilities* → *Clarity of Instructions*		
x											x													x	x	
x											x													x	x	
x											x													x	x	
										x														x	x	
								x	x															x	x	
								x	x															x	x	
								x	x															x	x	
								x	x															x	x	
x								x	x					x										x	x	
x	x																									
x	x																									
x	x																									
x	x																									

Company	Item	Publisher or Author	Comments
American Art Class Company	Pottery supplies and equipment		Art supplies
American Art Class Company	Kilns and wheels		Art supplies
Allyn and Bacon	Pageant of World History	Gerald Leinwand	History textbooks
Allyn and Bacon	Widening Views		Manual
Allyn and Bacon	High Trails		
American Book Company	167 books in reading series of books and study books		Reading series dealing with phonetics, related word and learning skills and comprehension
American Book Company	Triple 1 Series		
	1 Aim, Ask, and Act Level 1		
	1 Build, Belong and Believe Level 2		
	I Can, Compete, and Care Level 3		
	I Do, Dare, and Dream Level 4		
	I Earn, Explore, and Excel Level 5		
	I Find, Follow, and Finish Level 6		

Educable Retarded	Trainable Retarded	Cerebral Palsy Victim	Physically Handicapped	Partially Sighted	Blind	Hard-of-Hearing	Gifted	Primary	Intermediate	Junior High	Senior High	Free	Low	Medium	High	Make-It-Yourself	Visual Perception	Auditory Perception	Eye-Hand Coordination	Fine Finger Coordination	Gross Motor	Poor Sequencing	Other	Yes	No
			Child						*Age Group*				*Cost*				*Applicable for Pupils with These Learning Disabilities*							*Clarity of Instructions*	
x	x																								
x	x																								
										x				x										x	
										x				x										x	
										x				x										x	
x								x	x	x	x			x									x	x	
x									x														x	x	
x									x	x													x	x	
x									x	x													x	x	
x									x														x	x	
x									x														x	x	
x									x														x	x	

Company	Item	Publisher or Author	Comments
Allied Educational, Council	Fitzhugh Plus Program		Reading readiness Supplementary material Perceptual learning and understanding
	Spatial Organization Series		3 Workbooks
	Language and Number Series		5 Workbooks
American Book Company	Dandy Dog ABC Learning Activities		Workbooks
American Book Company	Dandy Dog "Just Ask"		Record—picture book
American Book Company	Ideas, Images, and I		Reading Texts 7 reading levels
American Book Company	Webster's New Elementary Dictionary		Not designed for any particular handicap; could be used by EMR students
American Book Company	Webster's New Practical School Dictionary		
American Book Company	Webster's New Student's Dictionary		Not designed for any particular handicap
American Crayon Company	Prang Instant Powder Tempera		Arts and Crafts material for all levels of education
American Crayon Company	Prang Finger Paint		Good colors
American Crayon Company	Prang Water Colors		22 different colors
American Crayon Company	Prang-Poster Pastello Pressed Colored Chalk Crayons		22 different colors

Educable Retarded	Trainable Retarded	Cerebral Palsy Victim	Physically Handicapped	Partially Sighted	Blind	Hard-of-Hearing	Gifted	Primary	Intermediate	Junior High	Senior High	Free	Low	Medium	High	Make-It-Yourself	Visual Perception	Auditory Perception	Eye-Hand Coordination	Fine Finger Coordination	Gross Motor	Poor Sequencing	Other	Yes	No
x	x	x	x	x			x	x															x	x	
x	x	x	x	x			x	x						x			x			x					
x	x	x	x	x			x	x						x			x			x				x	
x								x						x									x	x	
x								x	x					x									x	x	
x									x	x													x	x	
									x	x	x														
x									x	x	x												x	x	
									x	x	x														

Company	Item	Publisher or Author	Comments
American Crayon Company	Prang Crayoney Crayons		49 different colors
American Crayon Company	Prang Tempera Colors		33 different colors
American Crayon Company	Everyday Art Suggestions		Pamphlet published 3 times a year (free)
Ann Arbor Publishers	Workbooks	Smith and Smith	
	Writing Words; Word Attack Skills		Reading, writing
	4 Reading Words; 5 Reading Words		Spelling, listening
	Word Attack and Comprehension		Basic readiness skills and remedial aids
Appleton-Century-Crofts			Language series
	Actions		Designed for classroom use
	Compound Sentences		Small-group setting
			Simple to complex
	More Actions Objects		Concrete to abstract
	Prepositions Relationships		

Educable Retarded	Trainable Retarded	Cerebral Palsy Victim	Physically Handicapped	Partially Sighted	Blind	Hard-of-Hearing	Gifted	Primary	Intermediate	Junior High	Senior High	Free	Low	Medium	High	Make-It-Yourself	Visual Perception	Auditory Perception	Eye-Hand Coordination	Fine Finger Coordination	Gross Motor	Poor Sequencing	Other	Yes	No
x							x	x	x	x	x	x	x											x	
x								x	x																
x								x	x														x	x	
x								x	x														x	x	
x									x														x	x	
x	x							x	x														x	x	
x	x							x	x														x		
x	x							x	x														x		
x	x							x	x														x		

Company	Item	Publisher or Author	Comments
Educational Teacher Aids (E.T.A.)			Sensory training materials; self-descriptive
	T/A Basic Weight Tablets		
	Montessori Color Tablets-2nd set		
	Montessori Broad Stair		
	Montessori Thermal Cylinders		
	Skittles (use with Division Boards)		
	Montessori Pink Tower		
	Reading Readiness Set		
	Fabric Set		
	Touch Boards	Montessori	
	Counting Box and Spindles	Montessori	
	Sound Boxes	Montessori	
	Knobless Cylinders	Montessori	
	Tray and Cabinet of Geometric insets	Montessori	
	Large Geometric Solids	Montessori	
	Short Division Board	Montessori	
	Long Division Board	Montessori	
	Long Stair	Montessori	

Educable Retarded	Trainable Retarded	Cerebral Palsy Victim	Physically Handicapped	Partially Sighted	Blind	Hard-of-Hearing	Gifted	Primary	Intermediate	Junior High	Senior High	Free	Low	Medium	High	Make-It-Yourself (Cost)	Visual Perception	Auditory Perception	Eye-Hand Coordination	Fine Finger Coordination	Gross Motor	Poor Sequencing	Other	Yes	No	
x		x		x		x		x								$12.50									x	match and sort color recognition
x		x	x			x		x								$12.45	x		x		x				x	
x	x		x	x		x		x	x							$14.95	x		x	x	x				x	
x	x	x	x	x	x		x		x							$17.85									x	Thermal discrimination
																$ 2.95										
x	x	x	x	x	x		x		x	x						$13.50	x		x	x	x				x	size distinction
x		x	x					x								$10.20	x								x	
x	x							x								$ 3.75									x	Texture
x	x	x	x	x	x		x		x							$17.90 a set				x					x	Kinesthetic concept of written numbers
x	x	x	x	x	x		x		x							$14.50			x		x				x	
x	x	x	x	x	x				x							$18.00		x							x	
x	x	x	x	x	x		x		x							$35.00	x		x	x	x				x	
x	x	x	x	x			x		x							$95.00	x		x	x					x	
x	x	x	x	x	x		x		x							$19.95	x		x	x					x	
x								x		x						$ 9.90										
								x		x						$22.50										
x	x	x	x	x	x		x		x							$11.50	x		x	x					x	Size discrimination

Company	Item	Publisher or Author	Comments
Simplex	Simple object replacement		
Playskool	Color Cubes		Wooden color cubes
Halsam	Play Tiles		Pegboard with tiles
Garrard Press	The 10 Game	Dolch	Reading skills
Kohner	Hi-Q		Reading skills
Ed-U-Cards	Go-Together Lotto		Reading skills
Ed-U-Cards	Farm Lotto		Reading skills
Ed-U-Cards	ABC Lotto		Reading skills
Ed-U-Cards	The World About Us Lotto		Reading skills
Ed-U-Cards	What's Missing Lotto		Reading skills
Constructive Playthings	Jumbo Beads		Perceptual motor skills
Ed-U-Cards	Picture Dominoes		Game
Platt and Munk Ed.	Giant Alphabet Box		Pictures for each letter
Lauri Enterprises	Fit-a-Space Junior		4 rubber puzzles
Lauri Enterprises	Fit-a-Space		Puzzle
Constructive Playthings	Coordinating Lock Board		Locks, screws, bolts (4 x 8 board)
Constructive Playthings	Beaded Alphabet	Touch, Inc.	2 boxes; tactile letters; manuscript and cursive
Constructive Playthings	Giant Beaded Numbers	Touch Inc.	
Schackman	Number Learner		Squares fit over pegs

		Child						Age Group				Cost					Applicable for Pupils with These Learning Disabilities							Clarity of Instructions		
Educable Retarded	Trainable Retarded	Cerebral Palsy Victim	Physically Handicapped	Partially Sighted	Blind	Hard-of-Hearing	Gifted	Primary	Intermediate	Junior High	Senior High	Free	Low	Medium	High	Make-It-Yourself	Visual Perception	Auditory Perception	Eye-Hand Coordination	Fine Finger Coordination	Gross Motor	Poor Sequencing	Other	Yes	No	
x	x		x					x					x				x			x					x	Develop sense of design
x	x		x					x	x				x				x		x	x					x	Free-time activity
x	x		x	x			x	x	x				x				x		x	x				x		Beginning numbers
x			x	x			x	x	x				x											x		Free-time activity
x			x				x			x	x		x											x		Free-time activity
x	x	x	x	x				x					x				x							x		Matching
x	x	x	x	x				x					x				x							x		"
x	x	x	x	x				x					x				x							x		"
x	x	x	x	x				x					x				x							x		"
x	x	x	x	x				x					x				x							x		"
x	x	x	x	x	x		x	x					x				x		x	x				x		Reading readiness
x	x	x	x	x			x	x	x				x				x							x		Reading readiness
x	x	x	x	x			x	x					x				x							x		
x	x	x	x	x	x			x					x				x		x	x				x		
x	x	x	x	x	x			x					x				x	x						x		
x	x	x	x	x	x			x					x				x				x			x		
x	x			x	x					x	x		x											x		Tactile-kinesthetic
x	x			x	x			x	x				x											x		"
x	x	x	x	x	x			x					x				x	x						x		

Company	Item	Publisher or Author	Comments
Sifo	Wooden Inlay Puzzle		
Milton Bradley	Alphabet Poster Cards		Alphabet recognition
McGraw-Hill	Touch & Learn Books		
Weber Costello	Count To Ten	Wozencraft	Workbook
Instructo	Puppet Playmates		Cardboard life-size cutouts
Milton Bradley	Phonetic Word Wheel		Yellow disc, black lettering; interchangeable discs
Milton Bradley	Phonetic Word Analyzer		
Milton Bradley	Giant Size Synonym Poster Cards		30 cards
Milton Bradley	Giant Size Consonant Poster Cards		
Milton Bradley	Giant Size Homonym Poster Cards		
Milton Bradley	Beads & Laces		100 cubes, cyliner, and spheres
Instructo	Let's Learn Sequence		Box of many cards
Milton Bradley	Number Concept Cards		
Milton Bradley	Picture Word Builder		Matching pictures and words
Milton Bradley	Design Blocks		4 shapes, 6 colors
Ideal	Cubical Counting Blocks		

Trainable Retarded	Cerebral Palsy Victim	Physically Handicapped	Partially Sighted	Blind	Hard-of-Hearing	Gifted	Primary	Intermediate	Junior High	Senior High	Free	Low	Medium	High	Make-It-Yourself	Visual Perception	Auditory Perception	Eye-Hand Coordination	Fine Finger Coordination	Gross Motor	Poor Sequencing	Other	Yes	No	
x	x	x	x				x				x					x	x							x	
x	x	x	x				x				x													x	Beginning reading
x	x	x	x				x				x					x								x	Listening skills
x	x	x	x				x				x					x		x	x				x		Beginning number skills
x							x	x			x												x		Language development
						x	x	x			x											reading & spelling	x		
						x	x	x			x											"	x		
						x		x	x		x											vocabulary improvement	x		
x		x					x				x											beginning sounds	x		
						x	x	x			x											vocabulary improvement	x		
x	x	x	x				x				x					x		x	x					x	
x	x	x	x				x				x					x					x			x	
x							x								$2.00							beginning numbers		x	
	x						x	x							$ .60	x								x	
x	x	x	x				x								$2.00	x							x		
x	x	x					x				x													x	

Company	Item	Publisher or Author	Comments
Instructo	Seasons Spring and Summer		Flocked cutouts for reading readiness
	We Learn To Count		
	Visiting the Farm		
	A Day At The Zoo		
	Community Helpers At Work		
American Guidance Service	Peabody Language Kits		Wide range of materials
Judy Co.	Clock with Gears		Moveable hands
Judy Co.	Small Clock		Individual use
Learning Center	Plastic Clock		
Judy Co.	Number Idents		Heavy individual boards first
Judy Co.	Color Shapes		Color recognition, 144 pieces
Judy Co.	Place Value Tab Rack		1's, 10's, 100's; show the meaning of numbers
Judy Co.	Number-ite		Individual rectangle for each number of pegs to show how many
Judy Co.	100 Peg Board		Large board, 100 pegs; 4 colors
Judy Co.	Match-ettes		Puzzle-type; matching parts
Judy Co.	Place Value Peg Holder		1's, 10's, 100's; sticks to count
Judy Co.	Story Sets		Cardboard; Children cut out

Educable Retarded	Trainable Retarded	Cerebral Palsy Victim	Physically Handicapped	Partially Sighted	Blind	Hard-of-Hearing	Gifted	Primary	Intermediate	Junior High	Senior High	Free	Low	Medium	High	Make-It-Yourself	Visual Perception	Auditory Perception	Eye-Hand Coordination	Fine Finger Coordination	Gross Motor	Poor Sequencing	Other	Yes	No
x	x	x	x	x				x								$5.95							Organizing and communication skills	x	
x	x	x	x	x				x								$4.50							Math instruction		x
x	x							x								$4.50								x	
x	x							x								$5.95								x	
x	x							x								$4.95								x	
x	x	x	x	x			x	x	x							x							Oral language develop	x	
x	x	x	x	x				x	x					x											x
x	x	x	x	x				x	x				x			x									x
x								x	x				x												x
x		x	x	x				x	x					x		x							Beginning arithmetic		x
x	x							x					x			x	x		x	x					x
x								x	x				x				x								x
x	x	x		x				x					x				x								x
x	x	x		x				x	x					x			x								x
x	x	x	x	x				x						x											x
x									x					x											x
x	x		x	x				x						x									Language development		x

Company	Item	Publisher or Author	Comments
Judy Co.	See Quees		Reading readiness; oral communication
Judy Co.	Puzzle Inlays		Large Wooden Puzzles
Children's Press (F. A. Owen)	The True Science Library	Friskey, M.	Volume 1-12 high-interest, low-reading-level science material
Children's Press (F. A. Owen)	Science charts		
	Simple chemistry		
	Animals		
	Simple Machines		
	Plants		
	Light and Sound		
	Magnetism and Electricity		
	Air and Weather		
	Earth and Sky		
Children's Press (F. A. Owen)	Book 1 & 2 Primary Experiments		Book of science dittoes
Children's Press (F. A. Owen)	Book 1 middle-grade Experiments		Book of science dittoes
Children's Press (F. A. Owen)	Charts for Middle Grades		Plants, air, weather, earth

Educable Retarded	Trainable Retarded	Cerebral Palsy Victim	Physically Handicapped	Partially Sighted	Blind	Hard-of-Hearing	Gifted	Primary	Intermediate	Junior High	Senior High	Free	Low	Medium	High	Make-It-Yourself	Visual Perception	Auditory Perception	Eye-Hand Coordination	Fine Finger Coordination	Gross Motor	Poor Sequencing	Other	Yes	No
x	x	x	x	x				x						x									Language development	x	
x	x	x	x	x				x						x											x
x		x	x	x				x	x					x									Science	x	
x		x	x	x			x	x	x				x										Science concept	x	
x		x	x	x			x	x	x				x				"							x	
x		x	x	x			x	x	x				x				"							x	
x		x	x	x			x	x	x				x				"							x	
x		x	x	x			x	x	x				x				"							x	
x		x	x	x			x	x	x				x				"							x	
x		x	x	x			x	x	x				x				"							x	
x		x	x	x			x	x	x				x				"							x	
x		x	x	x			x	x	x				x											x	
x		x	x	x			x	x	x				x											x	
x		x	x	x			x	x	x				x											x	

Company	Item	Publisher or Author	Comments
Developmental Learning Materials	Small Parquetry		
DLM	Design Cards/Small Parquetry		
DLM	Large Parquetry		
DLM	Design Cards/Large Parquetry		
DLM	Tracing Paper Designs		
DLM	Pre-Writing Designs		
DLM	Design cards for Colored inch cubes		
DLM	Colored inch cubes		
DLM	Plain inch cubes		
DLM	Design cards for plain inch cubes		
DLM	Buzzer board pattern cards		(Morse code type)
DLM	Buzzer Board		
DLM	Animal Puzzles		Body concept
DLM	People Puzzles		Body concept
DLM	Seasonal Stencils		Plastic-coated cardboard
DLM	Clear Stencils		Clear plastic shapes
DLM	Farm and Transportation Stencils		Plastic-coated cardboard
DLM	Shapes Stencils		Plastic-coated cardboard

Educable Retarded	Trainable Retarded	Cerebral Palsy Victim	Physically Handicapped	Partially Sighted	Blind	Hard-of-Hearing	Gifted	Primary	Intermediate	Junior High	Senior High	Free	Low	Medium	High	Make-It-Yourself	Visual Perception	Auditory Perception	Eye-Hand Coordination	Fine Finger Coordination	Gross Motor	Poor Sequencing	Other	Yes	No
x	x	x	x	x				x	x			x					x		x	x				x	
x	x	x	x	x				x	x			x					x		x	x					x
x	x	x	x	x				x	x			x					x		x	x					x
x	x	x	x	x				x	x			x					x		x	x					x
x	x	x	x	x				x	x			x					x		x	x					x
x	x	x	x					x	x					x			x	x							x
x	x	x	x					x	x					x			x	x							x
x	x	x	x					x	x					x			x	x							x
x	x	x	x					x	x					x			x	x							x
x	x	x	x					x	x					x			x	x							x
x	x	x	x					x	x					x			x	x							x
x	x	x	x					x	x					x			x	x							x
x	x	x	x					x						x			x								x
x	x	x	x					x						x			x								x
x	x	x	x					x						x			x								x
x	x	x	x					x						x			x							x	
x	x	x	x					x						x			x								x
x	x	x	x					x						x			x							x	

Company	Item	Publisher or Author	Comments
DLM	Animal Stencils		Plastic-coated cardboard
DLM	Auditory Rhythm Band		
DLM	Auditory Training Familiar Sounds		Type and picture cards
DLM	Sequential Picture Cards III		5 sequences, 6 cards each
DLM	Lacing Cards		Cards and Faces
DLM	Parquetry Insert Boards		
DLM	Body Concept Ditto Masters		
DLM	Pegboard Designs		Box #1 Box #2
DLM	Pegboard & Pegs		
EduKaid	Count-a-line		Includes instruction book
Holt, Rinehart, & Winston	Sounds of Language Readers		
Holt, Rinehart, & Winston	Tradition and Change in Four Societies		Reading
Holt, Rinehart, & Winston	Comparative Economic Systems An Inquiry Approach		Reading
Holt, Rinehart, & Winston	Brown Bear, Brown Bear What Do You See?		Reading
Holt, Rinehart, & Winston	My School Book of Picture Stories	E. Mill	Reading
Holt, Rinehart, & Winston	Long Ago in Colonial Days	J. Johnson	Reading

Child: Educable Retarded	Trainable Retarded	Cerebral Palsy Victim	Physically Handicapped	Partially Sighted	Blind	Hard-of-Hearing	Gifted	Age Group: Primary	Intermediate	Junior High	Senior High	Cost: Free	Low	Medium	High	Make-It-Yourself	Learning Disabilities: Visual Perception	Auditory Perception	Eye-Hand Coordination	Fine Finger Coordination	Gross Motor	Poor Sequencing	Other	Clarity: Yes	No
x	x	x	x					x						x			x							x	
x	x	x	x	x				x						x				x							x
x	x	x	x	x				x						x			x	x							x
x	x	x	x	x				x						x			x					x		x	
x	x	x	x	x				x						x			x		x	x	x				x
x	x	x	x					x						x			x		x	x	x				x
x	x	x	x					x						x											x
x	x	x	x					x						x			x								x
x	x	x	x					x						x			x		x	x					x
x							x			x	x			x			x							x	
x		x					x	x	x					x			Reading							x	
							x			x	x			x			Social studies							x	
							x			x	x			x			Social studies							x	
x		x	x				x	x	x				x				Reading								x
		x	x				x	x					x				"								x
		x	x				x	x	x				x				"								x

Company	Item	Publisher or Author	Comments
Holt, Rinehart, & Winston	A Fox Story	A. Sollers	Reading
Holt, Rinehart, & Winston	The Proud Peacock		Reading
Holt, Rinehart, & Winston	Good Old Kristie	E. Brock	Reading
Holt, Rinehard & Winston	Dr. Frick and His Fractions	H. Ford	Arithmetic Series
Holt, Rinehart, & Winston	The Electric Eel	C. Coates	
Holt, Rinehart, & Winston	Working Wheels	H. Weber	
Holt, Rinehart & Winston	If You Can Count To 10	H. Fehr	Reading series
Holt, Rinehart & Winston	At Your Own Risk	L. Trout M. Flanigan	Unit, record and library
Holt, Rinehart & Winston	I've Got A Name	L. Trout	Unit, record and library
Holt, Rinehart & Winston	Larger Than LIfe	E. Stull D. Sharpe	Unit, record and library
Holt, Rinehart & Winston	Cities	E. Stull C. Greenfield	Unit, record and library
Teaching Resources	Sequential perceptual-motor exercises	Dubnoff School	Exercise sheets crayons
SRA	Lift-Off To Reading–The Basal Progressive Choice Reading Program		

Child								Age Group				Cost					Applicable for Pupils with These Learning Disabilities								Clarity of Instructions	
Educable Retarded	Trainable Retarded	Cerebral Palsy Victim	Physically Handicapped	Partially Sighted	Blind	Hard-of-Hearing	Gifted	Primary	Intermediate	Junior High	Senior High	Free	Low	Medium	High	Make-It-Yourself	(Disability)	Visual Perception	Auditory Perception	Eye-Hand Coordination	Fine Finger Coordination	Gross Motor	Poor Sequencing	Other	Yes	No
		x	x					x					x				Reading									x
		x	x					x					x				"									x
			x	x			x	x					x				"									
			x	x			x	x					x				"									
			x	x			x	x	x				x				"									
			x	x			x	x					x				"									
			x	x			x	x					x				"									
Culturally Disad.									x				x				Language arts								x	
"									x				x				Language arts								x	
"									x				x				Language arts								x	
"									x				x				Language arts								x	
x	x	x	x	x				x					x				Line concepts								x	
x		x	x	x			x	x	x				x				Developing reading skills								x	

Company	Item	Publisher or Author	Comments
SRA	Lift-Off to Reading Workbooks		
Teaching Resources	Perceptual Motor Development	Fairbanks-Robinson	
Teaching Resources	Perceptual Motor Teaching Materials	Erie Program	
SRA	Writing Skills Laboratory (11 lessons)		Part 1: Narration (laboratory approach to individual instruction)
World Wide Games	String Figures Book		
World Wide Games	Tangrams Puzzle Book		
Holt, Rinehart & Winston	Sounds & Patterns of Language		Beginning reading
Keith Clark efi electronic futures inc.	Lok Letters		1200 upper case
	Audio notebook & tapes		Beginning reading
Keith Clark	Lok Letters		1200 lower case
Community Playthings	Truck		Sturdy, wooden
Ideal	Number Concept Board		Arithmetic
Matrix Games	Charts with Wooden holder		Sequencing
Keystone View Co.	Stereo Reader Machine & Stereo Reader cards		
Judy Co.	Hundred board		
World Wide Games	Jet Billiards		
World Wide Games	Tangram Puzzle		

Child								Age Group				Cost					Applicable for Pupils with These Learning Disabilities							Clarity of Instructions	
Educable Retarded	Trainable Retarded	Cerebral Palsy Victim	Physically Handicapped	Partially Sighted	Blind	Hard-of-Hearing	Gifted	Primary	Intermediate	Junior High	Senior High	Free	Low	Medium	High	Make-It-Yourself	Visual Perception	Auditory Perception	Eye-Hand Coordination	Fine Finger Coordination	Gross Motor	Poor Sequencing	Other	Yes	No
x		x	x	x			x	x	x							x	Developing reading skills							x	
x	x	x	x	x			x	x							x		x	x	x	x	x	x		x	
x	x	x	x	x			x	x						x			x	x	x	x	x	x		x	
							x			x				x			Writing skills							x	
																$2.35									
																$1.35									
x	x	x	x					x	x					x			x	x						x	
x	x	x	x	x				x	x					x			x		x					x	
x		x	x	x	x			x	x					x										x	
x	x	x	x	x				x	x					x			x		x					x	
x	x	x	x	x				x						x							x				x
x	x	x	x	x			x						x												x
x	x	x	x	x				x					x									x			x
x		x	x	x				x	x				x				Language Development							x	
x		x	x	x				x	x				x											x	
x		x	x				x		x	x	x		x							x				x	
x		x					x	x	x				x							x				x	

Company	Item	Publisher or Author	Comments
World Wide Games	Dancing Doll		
World Wide Games	Mexican Balero		
World Wide Games	Marble football		
Creative Playthings	Balance Board		
Creative Playthings	Pitch Back		Sturdy; throw ball at net; returned
American Printing House for Blind	Relief U.S. Map		
Howe Press	Perkins Brailler		
U.S. Government Talking Books	Free matter (books, etc.)		
Phono-visual	Vowel Chart		
Milton Bradley	Calander		
Children's Press	The True Book Series	Friskey	Science; high interest, low reading level
Random House	Sights & Sounds (series)	Ray O'Neill	Series for reading improvement and enjoyment; includes book, tape to be heard with head sets, and teacher's manual
Mor-Pla	4-wheeled bus		Motor skills
Mor-Pla	4-wheeled scooter		Play toy
Bell & Howell	Language Master		14 separate card programs
Bell & Howell	Language Master Phonics Series Set B		

Child								Age Group				Cost					Applicable for Pupils with These Learning Disabilities							Clarity of Instructions	
Educable Retarded	Trainable Retarded	Cerebral Palsy Victim	Physically Handicapped	Partially Sighted	Blind	Hard-of-Hearing	Gifted	Primary	Intermediate	Junior High	Senior High	Free	Low	Medium	High	Make-It-Yourself	Visual Perception	Auditory Perception	Eye-Hand Coordination	Fine Finger Coordination	Gross Motor	Poor Sequencing	Other	Yes	No
x		x					x		x	x	x			x											x
x		x					x		x	x	x	x	x						x						x
x		x	x				x		x	x	x					x			x					x	
x	x	x	x	x			x	x							x	x				x				x	
x	x	x	x	x			x	x	x							x				x				x	
						x			x	x	x			x											x
						x		x	x	x	x			x										x	
						x		x	x	x	x			x											x
x		x	x	x				x	x					x					x					x	
x	x	x	x	x				x						x											x
x		x	x	x				x	x					x										x	
x		x	x	x					x							x	x							x	
x	x	x	x	x				x								x					x				x
x	x	x	x	x				x								x					x				x
x	x	x	x	x			x	x								x							Audio-visual		x
x	x	x	x	x			x	x								x							"		x

Company	Item	Publisher or Author	Comments
Community Playthings	Teeter Tawter		Wooden, sturdy
Field Enterprises	Cyclo-Teacher Learning		Programmed learning; for reinforcement, enrichment, and practice with World Book Encyclopedia
World Wide Games	Hand Shadows Book		
World Wide Games	Adi Board		Counting game
SRA	WORK (widening occupation roles kit)		
SRA	Occupational Exploration Kit		
SRA	The Job Ahead		Occupation Reading Series
SRA	The Job Ahead—Workbook series		Occupational Reading Series
St. Nicholas	Addition Board Apparatus		Arithmetic
St. Nicholas	Subtraction Board Apparatus		Arithmetic
Milton Bradley	Geometric Figures and Solids		Arithmetic
ETA	Montessori Sorting Box Combination		Sensory training; long box; 2 boxes of objects
ETA	Montessori Teen Board		Sturdy, wooden
Capricorn Books	Montessori For The Disadvantaged	R. C. Orem	Teacher reference
Capricorn Books	Montessori and the Special Child	R. C. Orem	Teacher reference
ETA	United States Map Puzzle		
Rand McNally & Co.	Which Way?	Pattison and Robbins	Book, activity book and teachers manual

Educable Retarded	Trainable Retarded	Cerebral Palsy Victim	Physically Handicapped	Partially Sighted	Blind	Hard-of-Hearing	Gifted	Primary	Intermediate	Junior High	Senior High	Free	Low	Medium	High	Make-It-Yourself	Visual Perception	Auditory Perception	Eye-Hand Coordination	Fine Finger Coordination	Gross Motor	Poor Sequencing	Other	Yes	No	
x	x	x	x				x									x					x				x	
							x	x	x	x	x					x							x			
																$ 1.35										
x		x	x				x	x	x							$10.95									x	
x		x	x					x	x							x									x	
x		x	x								x					x								x		
x		x	x								x					x								x		
x		x	x								x					x								x		
x			x				x	x	x							$ 3.40									x	
x			x				x	x	x							$ 3.35									x	
x	x	x	x	x	x		x	x	x								x		x						x	Colors and counting
x	x							x	x							$19.95	x		x	x					x	counting
x	x	x	x	x				x	x							$15.00	x		x						x	
																$ 4.95										
																$ 5.95										
x		x	x					x	x							$10.00	x		x						x	Direction, distance, location
x	x	x	x	x			x	x	x								Space relationship							x		Direction, distance, location

Company	Item	Publisher or Author	Comments
Rand McNally	How Far?	Pattison and Robbins	Book, activity book and teacher's manual
Rand McNally	Where?	Pattison and Robbins	Book, activity book and teacher's manual
ETA	Montessori cylinders		Sensory training; sturdy, wooden
ETA	Montessori locks and latches		Sturdy, wooden
ETA	Montessori Sound blocks		Sturdy, wooden
ETA	Abacus		Sturdy, wooden
ETA	Montessori manipulative materials		Hooks, buckles, ties, snaps, zipper
Eye Gate House	Occupational Education		9 filmstrips, 9 tapes
Eye Gate House	Car Care for Safety	Safe Car Education Instruction	7 filmstrips, tapes, booklets
Rand McNally & Co.	Color	Lepthien and Heintz	4 filmstrips, color cards
Rand McNally & Co.	Our American Flag	Lepthien and Heintz	31 page booklet
Rand McNally	Handbook of Map and Globe Usage	Harris	Teacher reference manual
Rand McNally	Map Activities in American History		Book 1, Book 11, workbook
Rand McNally	Many Nations: A Survey of the Countries of the World	Pearcy	
Eye Gate House	Discovery Trips Activity Book	Bate and Peterson	Sight and Sound

Child								Age Group				Cost					Applicable for Pupils with These Learning Disabilities							Clarity of Instructions	
Educable Retarded	Trainable Retarded	Cerebral Palsy Victim	Physically Handicapped	Partially Sighted	Blind	Hard-of-Hearing	Gifted	Primary	Intermediate	Junior High	Senior High	Free	Low	Medium	High	Make-It-Yourself	Visual Perception	Auditory Perception	Eye-Hand Coordination	Fine Finger Coordination	Gross Motor	Poor Sequencing	Other	Yes	No
x	x	x	x	x			x	x	x														Space relationship	x	
x	x	x	x	x			x	x	x														Space relationship	x	
x	x	x	x					x	x							$ 8.95	x		x	x	x	x			x
x	x	x	x					x	x							$ 8.95 apiece	x		x	x	x	x			x
x	x	x	x					x	x									x	x		x				x
x	x							x	x							$ 7.95	x		x	x					x
x	x	x	x	x				x	x							$ 4.95 apiece	x		x	x	x				x
x		x	x	x						x	x														x
x							x			x	x												Unit on car care and safety	x	
x	x							x															Awareness of differences (x)	x	
x		x	x	x			x	x	x														Unit on our country	x	
							x		x	x														x	
							x		x	x														x	
x	x							x									x		x	x				x	

17 pages

Company	Item	Publisher or Author	Comments
Eye Gate House	Captain Goodspeech and Mr. Mumbles	Sayre and Mack	6 filmstrips, sequence cards; 4 records
Eye Gate House	Captain Goodspeech, and Mr. Mumbles; teacher's edition	Sayre and Mack	
Eye Gate House	Think, Listen and Say; student/teacher edition	Sayre and Mack	4 sets of sequencing cards, and records
Eye Gate House	Getting To Know Me		6 filmstrips, 3 records
Eye Gate House	Let's Have Fun		4 filmstrips, 2 records
Eye Gate House	Story of the American Indian		9 filmstrips
Eye Gate House	Reading Readiness		10 filmstrips
SRA	Writing Skills Laboratory		Part 11, Description
SRA	Writing Skills Laboratory		Part 111 Exposition
SRA	Spelling word power	D. Parker F. Walker	
SRA	Reading Laboratory 1	D. Parker G. Scannell	
SRA	Word Games		Tests and keys
SRA	Math Symbols		Plastic numbers
SRA	Ten-Frame		Plastic frame
SRA	Discovery Board		
SRA	Handbook of Job Facts	N. Thiemann	Teacher reference
SRA	Our Working World: Families at Work	Senesh	Resource unit, recording, textbook, activity book

Educable Retarded	Trainable Retarded	Cerebral Palsy Victim	Physically Handicapped	Partially Sighted	Blind	Hard-of-Hearing	Gifted	(Child note)	Primary	Intermediate	Junior High	Senior High	Free	Low	Medium	High	Make-It-Yourself	Visual Perception	Auditory Perception	Eye-Hand Coordination	Fine Finger Coordination	Gross Motor	Poor Sequencing	Other	(Learning Disability note)	Yes	No
x	x							(Any speech impairment)	x	x										x		x				x	
x	x								x	x								x	x							x	
x	x	x			x	x		Hard of hearing										x	x						Listening skill	x	
x											x	x													Family living Sociology-guidance-sex education		x
x	x								x																Beginning science and math		x
x		x	x				x		x	x															American Indian Unit		x
x	x	x	x	x					x									x	x	x	x		x	x	Similarities		x
							x				x						x								Writing skills	x	
							x				x						x								Writing skills	x	
x							x		x	x							x								Phonetic approach	x	
x							x		x								x								Language skills	x	
x							x		x	x							x								Language skills	x	
x	x	x	x	x	x	x			x						x												x
	x	x	x						x						x												x
x		x	x	x					x						x											x	
x	x	x	x	x					x	x					x											x	

Company	Item	Publisher or Author	Comments
SRA	Our Working World		Resource unit, recording, textbook, activity book
SRA	Our Working World		Resource unit, recording, textbook, activity book
C. and E. Kruger	Walk the Doggie		Game for blind and sighted
G. Scott Educational Supply Co.	Master Cube		Wooden blocks; teach multiplication, addition, volume, ratio
American Printing House for Blind	Dymo Braille Tape Writer		
American Printing House for Blind	French Chess Set		Wooden frame; chessmen on pegs
Howe Press	Grooved Fiber Writing Cards		
	Alphabet Numeral Cards		
	Alluminum Signature Cards		
	Script Raised Alphabet		
	Square Hand Raised Alphabet		
American Printing House for Blind	Texas Slate and Type		Wooden frame; metal type
American Printing House for Blind	Staley Sports Field Kit		Metal boards; volleyball game baseball game, basketball game
American Printing House for Blind	Swail Dot Inverter Pad		

Educable Retarded	Trainable Retarded	Cerebral Palsy Victim	Physically Handicapped	Partially Sighted	Blind	Hard-of-Hearing	Gifted	Primary	Intermediate	Junior High	Senior High	Free	Low	Medium	High	Make-It-Yourself	Visual Perception	Auditory Perception	Eye-Hand Coordination	Fine Finger Coordination	Gross Motor	Poor Sequencing	Other	Yes	No
x	x	x	x	x				x	x					x										x	
x	x	x	x	x						x	x			x										x	
				x	x			x	x	x														x	
				x	x		x	x	x	x	x													x	
				x	x		x	x	x	x	x													x	
				x	x				x	x	x													x	
				x	x			x	x	x														x	
				x	x																			x	
				x	x																			x	
				x	x																				x
				x	x																				x
				x	x																				x
				x	x			x	x	x														x	
					x																			x	

Company	Item	Publisher or Author	Comments
American Printing House for Blind	Braille slate		
American Printing House for Blind	Cramer Abacus for Blind		Specially suited to needs of blind
Stevens Brothers Foundation	Templates for letter writing, signature cards and envelope addresser		
Howe Press	Dominoes		
C. & E. Kruger	Touch Aids: Number and Alphabet		
C. & E. Kruger	Touch Rings		Game in braille; inkprint for sighted
C. & E. Kruger	Run Mouse Run		Game for blind and sighted
United Church Press	Filmstrip and record: "A Family Affair"		Black-and-white film; child's life from birth to dating
Bremner Multiplication Records	Records—musical multiplication tables		Drills

| | | | | Child | | | | | Age Group | | | | Cost | | | | | Applicable for Pupils with These Learning Disabilities | | | | | | | Clarity of Instructions | |
Educable Retarded	Trainable Retarded	Cerebral Palsy Victim	Physically Handicapped	Partially Sighted	Blind	Hard-of-Hearing	Gifted	Primary	Intermediate	Junior High	Senior High	Free	Low	Medium	High	Make-It-Yourself	Visual Perception	Auditory Perception	Eye-Hand Coordination	Fine Finger Coordination	Gross Motor	Poor Sequencing	Other	Yes	No
				x	x																				
				x	x																			x	
				x	x																				
				x	x			x	x	x														x	
				x	x																				
				x	x			x	x	x	x													x	
				x	x		x	x	x	x														x	
x		x	x					x	x	x														x	
x		x	x	x	x			x	x	x							x							x	

VIII

PARTIAL INDEX OF COMPANIES PRODUCING MATERIALS FOR EXCEPTIONAL CHILDREN

A

Abbot Laboratories, North Chicago, Illinois, 60064.

Abelard-Schuman, Ltd., 6 West 57th Street, New York, New York, 10019.

Abingdon Press, 201 Eighth Avenue, South, Nashville, Tennessee, 37203.

Academic Media, Inc., 10835 Santa Monica Boulevard, Los Angeles, California, 90025 (Ted C. Clinard, Office Manager).

Academic Therapy Publications, 1543 Fifth Avenue, San Rafael, California, 94901.

Acme Visible Records, 5444 Bay Center Drive, Tampa, Florida, 33609.

Acousta Auditory Training Units, Inc., Rhode Island N. E., Albuquerque, New Mexico, 87110.

(The) Active Handicapped Magazine, 528 Aurora Avenue, Metairie, Lousiana, 70005.

Addison-Wesley, 106 West Station Street, Barrington, Illinois, 60010.

Addressograph Multigraph Corp., World Headquarters, 1200 Babbitt Road, Cleveland, Ohio, 44117.

Affiliated Publishers, 630 Fifth Avenue, New York, New York, 10020, (Division of Pocket Books, Inc.).

AIM Industries, Inc., 7841 Wayzata Blvd., Minneapolis, Minnesota, 55426.

Alda Instruments Ltd., 2444 Bloor Street West, Toronto, Ontario, Canada.
U. S. Representative: Harpster Audio Visual Equipment, Inc., 7777 Exchange Street, Cleveland, Ohio, 44125.

Alexander Graham Bell Association for the Deaf, 1537 35th Street, N. W., Washington, D. C., 20007.

Allen Company, 4200 Arbutus Court, Hayward, California, 94542 (Rep. Esther Carson).

Allied Education Council, Distribution Center, Box 78, Galien, Michigan, 49113.

Allyn & Bacon, Inc., 150 Tremont Street, Boston, Massachusetts 02122.

American Academy of Ophthalmology & Otolaryngology, 15 Second Street, S. W., Rochester, Minnesota, 55901.

American Annals of the Deaf, Gallaudet College, 7th Street and Florida Ave. N. E., Washington, D. C., 20002.

American Art Clay Company, Inc., 4717 West 16th Street, Indianapolis, Indiana, 46222.

American Association of Colleges for Teacher Education, 1201 Sixteenth Street, N. W., Washington, D. C., 20035.

American Association on Mental Deficiency, 20 North Street, Willimantic, Connecticut, 06226.

The American Bankers Association, 90 Park Avenue, New York, New York, 10016.

American Book Company, 300 Pike Street, Cincinnati, Ohio, 45202.

The American Cancer Society, 115 W. Oak Street, Bowling Green, Ohio, 43402.
National Headquarters, 521 W. 57th Street, New York, New York.

American Cleft Palate Association, Department of Communicative Disorders, College of Health-Related Professions, University of Florida, Gainesville, Florida, 32603.

American Crayon Company, 1708 Hayes Avenue, Sandusky, Ohio, 44870.

American Education Publications, Educational Center, 1250 Fairwood Avenue, Columbus, Ohio, 43216.

American Forest Products Industries, Inc., 1835 K Street, N. W., Washington, D. C., 20006.

American Foundation for the Blind, 15 West 16th Street, New York, New York, 10011.

American Guidance Service, Inc., Publishers Building, Circle Pines, Minnesota, 55014.

American Handicrafts Company, 4707 Euclid, Cleveland, Ohio, 44103 (Division of Tandy Corp.).

The American Iron & Steel Institute, Teaching Aids Distribution Center, Bedford Hills, New York.

The American Legion, Washington Office, 1608 K Street N. W., Washington, D. C., 20006.

American Library Association, 50 East Huron Street, Chicago, Illinois.

or

Weston Woods, Weston, Connecticut, 06883.

American Occupational Therapy Association 251 Park Avenue South, New York, New York, 10010.

American Plywood Association, 1119 "A" Street, Tacoma, Washington, 98401.

American Podiatry Association, 20 Chevy Chase Circle, N. W., Washington, D. C., 20015.

American Printing House for the Blind, Inc., 1839 Frankfort Avenue, Louisville, Kentucky, 40206.

American Psychological Association 1200 17th Street, N. W., Washington, D. C., 20036.

American Reedcraft Corp., 417 Lafayette Ave., Box 154, Hawthorne, New Jersey, 07506.

American School for the Deaf, 139 North Main Street, West Hartford, Connecticut, 06107.

American Seating, Grand Rapids, Michigan

or

2850 N. W. 31st Street, Portland, Oregon, 97210.

American Speech and Hearing Association, 9030 Old Georgetown Road, Washington, D. C., 20014.

The American Southern Publishing Co., Northport, Alabama, 35476.

American Thermoform Corp., 1732 West Slauson Avenue, Los Angeles, California.

American Trucking Association, Inc., 1616 P Street N. W., Washington, D. C., 20036.

American Wood Council, 200 Clayton Street, Denver, Colorado, 80206.

Paul S. Amidon & Associates, Inc., 5408 Chicago Avenue South, Minneapolis, Minnesota, 55417.

Ann Arbor Publications, 610 South Forest Avenue, Ann Arbor, Michigan, 48104.

Anthony School Equipment Co., 1603 East Olive Street, P. O. Box 552, Milwaukee, Wisconsin, 53211.

Anti-Defamation League of B'nai B'rith, 315 Lexington Avenue, New York, New York, 10016.

Appleton-Century-Crofts, 440 Park Avenue South, New York, New York, 10016.

Argus Communications, 3505 Ashland Avenue N., Chicago, Illinois, 60657.

Associated School Distributors, Inc., 220 West Madison Street, Chicago, Illinois.

ASCD, 1201 16th Street N. W., Washington, D. C., 20036.

Atherton Press, 70 5th Avenue, New York, New York, 10011.

Audio Applications, Educational Division, 78 East Palisade Avenue, Englewood, New Jersey, 07631.

Audio Dynamic Research, 1219 East 11th Street, Pueblo, Colorado, 81001.

Audio-Visual Supply Company, 527 S. W. Hall, Portland, Oregon, 97200.

Automobile Manufactures Association, Inc., 320 New Center Building, Detroit, Michigan, 48202.

AVID Corporation, P. O. Box 4263, 10 Tripps Lane, E. Providence, Rhode Island, 02914.

B

B & J Photo Service, 525 N. Main Street, P. O. Box 675, Findlay, Ohio, 45840.

Basic Books, Inc., 404 Park Avenue South, New York, New York, 10016.

Beckley-Cardy Company, 1900 N. Narragansett Ave., Chicago, Illinois, 60639.

Behavior Today, P. O. Box 2994, Boulder, Colorado, 80302.

Behavioral Research Laboratories, 3139 Dorris Avenue, Columbus, Ohio, 43202.

Bell & Howell Company, 7100 McCormick Road, Chicago, Illinois, 60645.

Benefic Press, 1900 North Narragansett, Chicago, Illinois, 60639.

Chas. A. Bennett Co., Inc., 809 West Detweiller Drive, Peoria, Illinois, 61614.

Robert Bently, Inc., 872 Massachusetts Avenue, Cambridge, Massachusetts, 02139.

Benton Review Publishing Company, Fowler, Indiana, 47944.

Berlow-Shillig-Speckert, Inc., 1320 Blueberry Lane, Charlotte, North Carolina, 28211.

Channing L. Bete Co., Inc., 45 Federal Street, Greenfield, Massachusetts, 01301.

Dick Blick, P. O. Box 1267, Galesburg, Illinois, 61401.

Binney & Smith, 380 Madison Avenue, New York, New York, 10017.

BLU-RAY, Inc. Essex, Connecticut, 06426.

The Bobbs-Merrill Company, Inc., 4300 West 62nd Street, Indianapolis, Indiana, 46206.

Bolt Beranek and Newman Inc. *See:* Honor Products Co.

Book-Lab, Inc., 1449 37th Street, Brooklyn, New York, 11218.

Books on Exhibit, Mount Kisco, New York, New York, 10549.

R. R. Bowker Company, 1180 Avenue of the Americas, New York, New York, 11036.

Bowmar Records, Inc., 622 Rodier Drive, Glendale, California, 91201.

Stanley Bowmar Company, Inc., 12 Cleveland Street, Valhalla, New York, 10595.

Boy Scouts of America, Supply Division, New Brunswick, New Jersey, 08903.

Milton Bradley, Springfield, Massachusetts, 01101.

The Bratton Corp., 1105 Dublin Road, Columbus, Ohio.

Bremner Multiplication Records, 161 Green Bay Road, Wilamett, Illinois, 60091.

Bro-Dart, 56 Earl Street, Newark, New Jersey, 07114.

Wm. C. Brown Company Publishers, 135 South Locust, Dubuque, Iowa, 52001.

Brown Shoe Company, 4327 Gustine Avenue, St. Louis, Missouri, 63116.

Bruce Publishing Company, 400 North Broadway, Milwaukee, Wisconsin, 53201.

Bureau of Auditory Education, 1612 Lyman Place, Hollywood, California, 90027.

Burgess Publishing Company, 424 South 6th Street, Minneapolis, Minnesota, 55415.

Business Equipment Center, Inc., 941 West 7th, Eugene, Oregon, 97402.

Business Forms, Inc., P. O. Box 552, Golden Colorado, 80401.

C

John D. Caddy, Box 251, Canoga Park, California, 91305.

Caedmon Records, Inc., 505 Eighth Avenue, New York, New York, 10018.

California Redwood Association, 617 Montgomery Street, San Francisco, California, 94111.

California Test Bureau, Del-Monte Research Park, Monterey, California, 93940.

University of California, Extension Media Center, Berkeley, California, 94720.

Campbell Films, Saxtons River, Vermont, 05154.

Canadian Folk Dance Service, 605 King Street W., Toronto 2B, Canada.

Carousel Films, Inc., 1501 Broadway, New York, New York, 10036.

Esther Carson, 18623 Lake Chabot Road, Castro Valley, California, 94546.

Catholic University of America Press, 620 Michigan Avenue, N. E., Washington, D. C., 20017.

CEBCO/STANDARD PUBLISHING, P. O. Box 31138, Cincinnati, Ohio, 45231.

Cenco Educational Aids, 1700 Irving Park Road, Chicago, Illinois, 60613.

Cereal Institute, Inc., 135 South La Salle Street, Chicago, Illinois, 60603.

Chandler Publishers, 124 Spear Street, San Francisco, California, 94105.

Cheviot Corporation, Department M 671, Box 34485, Los Angeles, California, 90034.

University of Chicago Press, 11030 S. Langley Avenue, Chicago, Illinois, 60628.

Child Guidance Toys, P. O. Box 113, Bronx, New York, 10472.

Child Study Association of America, Inc., Publications Department, 9 East 89th Street, New York, New York, 10028.

Childcraft Equipment Co., Inc., 155 East 23rd Street, New York, New York, 10010.

Childcraft Education Corp., 964 Third Street, New York, New York, 10022.

Children's Music Center, Inc., 5373 West Pico Boulevard, Los Angeles, California, 90019.

Children's Press, Inc., 1224 West Van Buren Street, Chicago, Illinois, 60607.

Chronicle Guidance Publications, Inc., Moravia, New York, 13118.

Clem Williams Films Inc., 2240 Noblestown Road, Pittsburgh, Pennsylvania, 15205.

Cleveland District Dairy Council, 504 Central Medical Arts Building, 2475 E. 22nd Street, Cleveland, Ohio, 44115.

Cleveland Leather Company, 2824 Lorain Avenue, Cleveland, Ohio, 44113.

Cleveland Public Library, Talking Book Service, 325 Superior Avenue, Cleveland, Ohio, 44114 (Katherine Prescott).

Collier-MacMillan Distribution Center, Collier-MacMillan Library Service, P. O. Box 2472, Church Street Station, New York, New York, 10008.

Columbia University, Teachers College, 525 West 120 Street, New York, New York, 10027.

The Combined Book Exhibit, Thomas J. McLaughlin, Director, Scarborough Park, Albany Post Road, Briarcliff Manor, New York, 10510.

Community Playthings, Rifton, New York, 12471.

Charles E. Conrad Films, 6331 Weidlake Drive, Hollywood, California, 90028.

Conservation Districts Foundation, P. O. Box 776, League City, Texas.

Colonial Films, Inc., 752 Spring Street, N. W., Atlanta, Georgia, 30308.

Colorado Association for Retarded Children, 1540 Vine Street, Denver, Colorado, 80206.

Columbia Ribbon & Carbon Manufacturing Co., Inc., 10150 W. Nine Mile Road, Oak Park, Michigan, 48237.

Constructive Playthings, 1040 East 85th, Kansas City, Missouri, 64131.

Continental Press, Inc., Elizabethtown, Pennsylvania, 17022.

Control Development, Inc., 1712 South Clifton Ave., Park Ridge, Illinois, 60068.

David C. Cook Publishing Co., Public & Private School Division, Elgin, Illinois, 60120.

Copia Manufacturing Corp., 1055 Stewart Avenue, Garden City, New York, 11530.

Coronet Films, 65 East South Water Street, Chicago, Illinois, 60601

Council for Exceptional Children, N. E. A., 1201 16th Street N. W., Washington, D. C., 20036.

Cousino Visual Education Service, 1945 Franklin Avenue, Toledo, Ohio, 43601.

Coward-McCann, Inc., 200 Madison Avenue, New York, New York, 10016.

CPC International, International Plaza, Englewood Cliffs, New Jersey, 07632.

George F. Cram Co., Inc., 301 S. LaSalle, Indianapolis, Indiana.

Creative Ideas, Co., Tooties Division, 5328 West 142nd Street, Hawthorne, California, 90250.

Creative Playthings, Inc., Edinburg Road, Cranbury, New Jersey, 08512.

Creative Scope, Inc., 509 Fifth Avenue, New York, New York, 10017.

CCM School Materials, Inc., (Crowell, Collier, and Macmillan, Inc.), 2124 West 82nd Place, Chicago, Illinois, 60620.

Cuisenaire Company of America, Inc., 12 Church Street, New Rochelle, New York, 10805.

Current Affairs Films, 527 Madison Avenue, New York, New York, 10022.

Curriculum Materials Corp., 119 South Roach Street, Jackson Mississippi, 39205.

Cybernetics Research Institute (C/R/I), 2233 Wisconsin Avenue, N. W., Washington, D. C., 20007.

D

A. Daigger & Co., Inc., Educational Teaching Aids Division (E. T. A.), 159 Kinzie Street, Chicago, Illinois, 60610.

John Day Company, Inc., 62 West 45th Street, New York, New York, 10036.

Delco Craft Center, Inc., 30081 Stephenson Highway, Madison Heights, Michigan, 48071.

Dell Publishing Company, Inc., 750 Third Avenue, New York, New York, 10017.

Dembar Educational Research Services (D. E. R. S.), P. O. Box 1605, Madison, Wisconsin, 53701.

T. S. Denison & Co., Inc., 321 Fifth Avenue South, Minneapolis, Minnesota, 55415.

Denoyer-Geppert, 5235 Ravenswood Avenue, Chicago, Illinois, 60640.

Department of Transportation, Federal Aviation Administration, Washington, D. C., 20590.

Developmental Learning Materials, 3505 North Ashland Ave., Chicago, Illinois, 60657.

The Devereux Foundation, Devon, Pennsylvania, 19333.

Di-Bur, Box 1184, Pueblo, Colorado, 81002.

Didactics Corp., 700 Grace Street, Mansfield, Ohio, 44905.

Digital Equipment Corp., 146 Main Street, Maynard, Massachusetts, 01754.

Dimensions in Early Learning, P. O. Box 4221, San Rafael, California, 94903.

Diocese of Columbus, 80 South Sixth Street, Columbus, Ohio, 43215.

Walt Disney Films, Midwest Office, 666 Busse Highway, Park Ridge, Illinois, 60068.
Home office: 800 Sonora Avenue, Glendale, California, 91201.

Diversified Business Equipment, 1745 Sylvania Avenue, Toledo, Ohio, 43613.

Doubleday & Company, Inc., Garden City, Long Island, New York, 11531.

DuKane Corporation, Audio Visual Division, St. Charles, Illinois, 60174.

E. P. Dutton and Co., Inc., 201 Park Avenue South, New York, New York, 10003.

E

Eberhard Faber, Wilkes-Barre, Pennsylvania, 18703.

Eckstein Brothers, 4807 West 118th Place, Hawthorne, California, 90250.

The Economy Company, Indianapolis, Indiana, 46206.

Edmund Scientific Co., 402 Edscorp Building, Barrington, New Jersey, 08007.

Educational Activities, Inc., Box 392, Freeport, Long Island, New York, 11520.

Educational Developmental Laboratories, 284 East Pulaski Road, Huntington, New York, 11743 (Division of McGraw-Hill Book Co.).

Educational Equipment Research & Manufacturing Co. (EERAM), 7296 Hillandale, Chesterland, Ohio, 44026.

Educational Innovations, Inc., 203 N. Fourth Street, Carrollton, Illinois, 62016.

Educational Media Selection Centers, National Book Committee, Inc., One Park Avenue, New York, New York, 10016.

Educational Products Information Exchange Institute (EPIE), 386 Park Avenue South, New York, New York, 10016.

Educatioal Projections Corp., P. O. Box 1187, 527 South Commerce Street, Jackson, Mississippi, 39205.

Educational Record Sales, 157 Chambers Street, New York, New York, 10007.

Educational Recordings of America, Inc., P. O. Box 6062, Bridgeport, Connecticut, 06606.

Educational Research Associates, Inc., P. O. Box 6604, Philadelphia, Pennsylvania, 19149.

Educational Resources, Inc., 2320 West Peterson Avenue, Chicago, Illinois, 60645.

Educational Service, Inc., P. O. Box 219, Stevensville, Michigan, 49127.

Educational Solutions, Inc., P. O. Box 190, Cooper Station, New York, New York, 10003.

Educational Teaching Aids (E. T. A.), A. Daigger & Co., Inc., 159 West Kinzie Street, Chicago, Illinois, 60610.

Educators Publishing Service, 301 Vassar Street, Cambridge, Massachusetts, 02139.

Edukaid of Ridgewood, 1250 East Ridgewood Avenue, Ridgewood, New Jersey, 07450.

Electro Systems, Inc., 847 South High Street, Columbus, Ohio, 43206.

EMC Corporation, Educational Materials Division, 180 East 6th Street, St. Paul, Minnesota, 55101.

Encyclopaedia Britannica Educational Corp., 425 N. Michigan Avenue, Chicago, Illinois, 60611,
        or
3450 W. Central, Toledo, Ohio, 43611.

The Epilepsy Foundation, 1419 "H" Street, N. W., Washington, D. C., 20005.

Expression Co., P. O. Box 11, Magnolia, Massachusetts, 01930.

Eye Gate House, Inc., 146-01 Archer Avenue, Jamaica, New York, 11435,
  or
14951 Birwood, Detroit, Michigan, 48238.

F

Farrar, Straus and Giroux, Inc., 19 Union Square West, New York, New York, 10003

Fearon Publishers, 2165 Park Boulevard, Palo Alto, California, 94306.

Field Educational Publications, Inc., 609 Mission Street, San Francisco, California, 94105.

Field Enterprises Educational Corporation, Educational Services, Station 8, Merchandise Mart Plaze, Chicago, Illinois, 60654.

Films Incorporated, 1144 Wilmette Avenue, Wilmette, Illinois, 60091.

The Fine Arts Recording Co., Inc., 255 Flowler Road, Westminster, Maryland, 21157.

Finney Company, 3350 Gorham Avenue, Minneapolis, Minnesota, 55426.

First Aid for Teachers, Box 4232, Denver, Colorado, 80204.

Florida Citrus Commission, School Services Department, Lakeland, Florida.

Robert Friedman Associates, 24800 Chagrin Boulevard, Cleveland, Ohio, 44122.

Friendship Press. 475 Riverside Drive, Room 753, New York, New York, 10027.

Ful-Vu Visuals, 1625 East End Avenue, Chicago Heights, Illinois, 60411.

GAF Corporation, Industrial Products Division, Glenville Station, Greenwich, Connecticut, 06830.

Folkways Scholastic Records, 906 Sylvan Avenue, Englewood Cliffs, New Jersey, 07632.

Follett Publishing Company, P. O. Box 5705, Chicago, Illinois, 60680.

Ford Motor Company, The American Road, Dearborn, Michigan, 48121.

Forest Press, Inc. of Lake Placid, Club Education Foundation, Lake Placid Club, New York, 12946.

G

Gager's Handicraft, 1024 Nicollet Avenue, Minneapolis, Minnesota, 55403.

Garrard Publishing Company, Champaign, Illinois, 61820.

General Binding Sales Corp., 3455 Dorr Street, Room 3, Toledo, Ohio, 43608, (Dan Smith, Representative).

General Electric Co., P. O. Box 831, Utica, New York.

General Learning Corporation, Early Learning Division, 3 East 54th Street, New York, New York, 10022.

General Programmed Teaching, Div. of Commerce Clearing House, Inc., 424 University Avenue, P. O. Box 402, Palo Alto, California, 94302.

G. W. School Supply Specialists (Geography Work Book Co.), 5626 East Belmont Avenue, P. O. Box 14, Fresno, California, 93707.

J. K. Gill Co., School & Wholesale Division, 1003 Lenora, Seattle, Washington.

Ginn & Company, 72 Fifth Avenue, New York, New York, 10011.

Globe Book Company, Inc., 175 Fifth Avenue, New York, New York, 10011.

Go-Mo, Box 142, Waterloo, Iowa, 50704.

Goodyear Tire and Rubber Corp., Akron, Ohio, 44316.

Grolier Educational Corporation, Spencer Division, 845 Third Avenue, New York, New York, 10022.

Grosset & Dunlap, Inc., 51 Madison Avenue, New York, New York, 10010

Grune and Stratton, Inc., 381 Park Avenue, South, New York, New York, 10016.

The Gryphon Press, 220 Montgomery Street, Highland Park, New Jersey, 08904.

Guidance Associates, Harcourt, Brace & World, Pleasantville, New York, 10570.

H

The Hancrafters, Waupun, Wisconsin, 53963.

Harcourt, Brace & World, 757 Third Avenue, New York, New York, 10017.

Harper & Row, Publishers, 49 East 33rd Street, New York, New York, 10016.

Harpster Audio Visual Equipment, Inc., 7777 Exchange Street, Cleveland, Ohio, 44125.

H. C. Electronics, Inc., Belvedere-Tiburon, California, 94920.

E. M. Hale & Co., Eau Claire, Wisconsin, 54701.

Hamilton Watch Company, Lancaster, Pennsylvania.

J. L. Hammett Co., 2393 Vauxhall Rd., Union, New Jersey, 07083.

C. S. Hammond and Company, Maplewood, New Jersey, 07040.

John Hancock Mutual Life Insurance Co., 200 Berkeley Street, Boston Massachusetts, 02117.

Harris County Center for the Retarded, Inc., 3550 West Dallas, P. O. Box 13403, Houston, Texas, 77019.

Delmer F. Harris Co., P. O. Box 288, Concordia, Kansas, 66901.

Hayes School Publishing Co., Inc., 321 Pennwood Ave., Wilkins-burg, Pennsylvania, 15221.

D. C. Hearth & Company, Boston, Massachusetts, 02116.

Highlights for Children, P. O. Box 269, Columbus Ohio.

R. H. Hinkley Co., 575 Lexington Ave., New York, New York, 10022.

Hoctor Records, Waldwick, New Jersey, 07463.

J. R. Holcomb & Co., 3000 Quigley Road, Cleveland, Ohio, 44113.

Holiday House, 18 East 56th Street, New York, New York, 10022.

Holt, Rinehart, & Winston, Inc. 383 Madison Avenue, New York, New York, 10017.

Honor Products Company, Division of Bolt, Beranek & Newman, Inc., 50 Moulton Street, Cambridge, Massachusetts, 02138.

Hoover Brothers, Inc., 1305 North 14th Street, Temple, Texas, 76501.

The Johns Hopkins Press, Baltimore, Maryland, 21218.

Houghton-Mifflin Co., 53 West 43rd Street, New York, New York, 10036.

Howe Press of Perkins School for the Blind, Watertown, Massachusetts, 02172.

The Hubbard Co. & the Ward Division, P. O. Drawer 100, Defiance, Ohio, 43512.

I

I T A Publications, Inc., 20 East 46th Street, New York, New York, 10017.

Ideal School Supply Co., 11000 South Lavergne Avenue, Oak Lawn, Illinois, 60453.

University of Illinois Press, Urbana, Illinois, 61801.

Imperial Productions, Inc., Educational Division, Kankakee, Illinois, 60901.

Incentives for Industry, 4529 Monroe Street, Toledo, Ohio, 43613.

Indiana University Press, 10th and Morton Streets, Bloomington, Indiana, 47401.

The Indianapolis Speech and Hearing Center, 615 North Alabama Street, Indianapolis, Indiana, 46202.

Initial Teaching Alphabet Publications, Inc., 20 East 46th Street, New York, New York, 10017.

Institute of Educational Research, Inc., 2900 "M" Street, N. W., Washington, D. C., 20007.

The Instructional Fair, Box 6190, Grand Rapids, Michigan, 49506.

Instructive Devices, Inc., 147 Armistice Blvd., Pawtucket, Rhode Island, 02860.

Instructo Corporation, Paoli, Pennsylvania, 19301.

The Instructor Publications, Inc., Dansville, New York, 14437.

Interculture Associates, Box 277, Thompson, Connecticut, 06277.

International Business Machines Corp., 1812 Madison Avenue, Toledo, Ohio, 43624.

International Communication Films, 1371 Reynolds Avenue, Santa Ana, California, 92705 (Division of Doubleday & Co.).

International Paper Company, P.O. Box 2328, Mobile, Alabama, 36601.

International Reading Association, Box 119, Six Tyre Avenue, Newark, Delaware, 19711.

International Society for Rehabilitation of the Disabled, 219 East 44th Street, New York, New York, 10017.

Interstate Printers and Publishers, Inc., 19-27 North Jackson Street, Danville, Illinois, 61832.

University of Iowa, Special Education Curriculum Development Center, Iowa City, Iowa, 52240.

J

Keith Jennison Books/Franklin Watts, Inc., Division of Grolier Inc., 575 Lexington Avenue, New York, New York, 10022.

The Judy Company, 310 North 2nd Street, Minneapolis, Minnesota, 55401.

K

Kayette Sales, 229 "O" Street, Willis Day Industrial Park, Perrysburg, Ohio, 43551.

Kellogg Company, Battle Creek, Michigan, 49016.

Kenworthy Educational Service, Inc., P. O. Box 3031, Buffalo, New York,

Keuffel & Esser Co., 2505 Industrial Row, Troy, Michigan, 48084.

Keystone View Company, Meadville, Pennsylvania, 16335.

Kimberly-Clark Corporation, Neenah, Wisconsin, 54956.

The King Company, 2414 W. Lawrence Avenue, Chicago, Illinois, 60625.

Kleeco Publishing Incorporated, 600 W. Jackson Boulevard, Chicago, Illinois, 60606.

Knowledge Aid, Division of Radiant Corporation, 8220 North Austin Avenue, Morton Grove, Illinois, 60063.

L

Ladoca Project & Publishing Foundation, Inc., East 51st Avenue & Lincoln Street, Denver, Colorado, 80216.

Lakeshore Equipment Co. PO Box 2116, 1144 Montague Avenue, San Leandro, California, 94577.

Landmark Productions, Inc., 1600 Broadway, New York, New York, 10019.

Larbar Corporation, Box 224, St. Paul, Minnesota, 55102.

Laubach, Literacy, Inc., Box 131, Syracuse, New York, 13210.

Gary D. Lawson, 9488 Sara Street, Elks Grove, California, 95624.

Lea & Febiger, Washington Square, Philadelphia, Pennsylvania, 19106.

Learn-X Corporation, Lake City, Minnesota, 55041.

Learning Pathways, Inc., 1028 Acoma Street, Denver, Colorado, 80204.

Learning Systems Press, PO Box 64, Urbana, Illinois, 61801.

J. B. Lippincott Co., East Washington Square, Philadelphia, Pennsylvania, 19105.

Little, Brown and Company, 34 Beacon Street, Boston, Massachusetts, 02106.

Lok-Letters, Union & Division Streets, Sidney, New York, 13838.

Love Publishing Co., 6635 East Villanova Place, Denver, Colorado, 80222.

The Ludy Co., R. R. # 2 Center Ridge, Arkansas, 72027.

Lyons & Carnahan, 407 East 25th Street, Chicago, Illinois, 60616.

Lyons Band Instrument Co., Inc., 223 W. Lake Street, Chicago, Illinois, 60606.

M

The Macmillan Company, School Department, 866 Third Avenue, New York, New York, 10022.

Mafex Associates, Inc., Box 519, Johnstown, Pennsylvania, 15907.

Magnetic Aids, Inc., 11 West 42nd Street, New York, New York, 10036.

J. A. Majors Company, PO Box 1690, Atlanta, Georgia, 30303.

Manca Press, Inc., PO Box 1343, Tulso, Oklahoma, 74101.

Marlon Creations, Inc., 29-04 37th Avenue, Long Island City, New York, 11101.

Materials for Learning Inc., Dept. 62, 1078 St. Johns Place, Brooklyn, New York, 11213.

Mattel, Inc., 5150 Rosecrans Avenue, Hawthorne, California, 90250.

Charles Mayer Studios, Inc., 776 Commins Street, Akron, Ohio, 44307.

McGraw-Hill Book Company, 330 West 42nd Street, New York, New York, 10036.

McGraw-Hill Book Company, Webster Division, Manchester Road, Manchester, Missouri, 63011.

McGraw-Hill, Educational Developmental Laboratories, Inc., Huntington, New York.

McGraw-Hill Films, 330 West 42nd Street, New York, New York, 10036.

David McKay Company, Inc., 750 Third Avenue, New York, New York, 10017.

McKnight & McKnight Publishing Co., U. S. Route 66 at Towanda Avenue, Bloomington, Illinois, 61701.

Mead Educational Services, 245 North Highland Avenue, N. E., Atlanta, Georgia, 30307.

Media, P. O. Box 2005, Van Nuys, California, 91404.

Meredith Press, 1716 Locust Street, Des Moines, Iowa, 50303.

Charles E. Merrill Publishing Co., 1300 Alum Creek Drive, Columbus, Ohio, 43216.

Merry Madison Handicrafts, 500 W. Florida Street, P. O. Box 5332, Milwaukee, Wisconsin, 53204.

Metric Association, Inc., 2004 Ash Street, Waukegan, Illinois, 60085.

Michigan State University, College of Education, Erickson Hall, East Lansing, Michigan, 48823.

Microcard Editions, Inc., Dept. G, 901- 26th Street, N. W., Washington, D. C., 20037.

Joseph Miller Books, 409 San Pasqual Drive, Alhambra, California, 91801.

Milliken Publishing Co., F & S Enterprises, 1012 East Dorothy Lane, Dayton, Ohio, 45419.

Milton Brakley Co., Springfield, Massachusetts, 01101.

3 M Company, Business Products Sales Inc., 4215 Monroe Street, Toledo, Ohio, 43606.

MKM Inc., 809 Kansas City Street, Rapid City, South Dakota, 57701.

Modern Teaching Associates, Inc., 1506 West Pierce Street, Milwaukee, Wisconsin, 53246.

Moody Institute of Science, Educational Film Division, 12000 E. Washington Blvd., Whittier, California, 90606.

Morgan Adhesive Company, 4560 Darrow Road, Stow Ohio.

Motion Picture Enterprises Publications, Inc., Tarrytown, New York, 10591.

Motivational Research, Inc., P. O. Box 140, McLean, Virginia, 22101.

N

NASCO, Fort Atkinson, Wisconsin, 53538.

National Aid to Visually Handicapped, 3201 Balboa Street, San Francisco, California, 94121.

National Association for Retarded Children, Inc., 420 Lexington Ave., New York, New York, 10017.

National Association of Hearing & Speech Agencies, 919 18th Street, N. W., Washington, D. C., 20006.

National Association of Sheltered Workshops, & Homebound Programs, 1522 "K" Street, N. W., Suite 410, Washington, D. C., 20005.

National Association of the Deaf, 2025 Eye Street, N. W., Suite 318, Washington, D. C., 20006.

National Audio-Visual Association, Inc., 3150 Spring Street, Fairfax, Virginia, 22030.

National Center for Audio Tapes, Bureau of Audio-Visual Instruction, Tape Duplication Service, Stadium Building, University of Colorado, Boulder, Colorado, 80302.

The National Cotton Council of America, P. O. Box 12285, Memphis, Tennessee, 38112.

National Cystic Fibrosis Research Foundation, 202 East 44th Street, New York New York , 10017.

National Dairy Council, 111 North Canal Street, Chicago, Illinois, 60606.

National East Seal Society for Crippled Children and Adults, 2023 West Ogden Avenue, Chicago, Illinois, 60612.

National Education Association, 1201 16th Street N. W., Washington, D. C., 20036.

National Geographic Society, P. O. Box 2118, Washington, D. C., 20013.

National Rehabilitation Association, 1522 "K" Street, N. W., Washington, D. C., 20005.

National Society for Crippled Children and Adults, 2023 West Ogden Avenue, Chicago, Illinois, 60612.

National Wildlife Federation, 1412 Sixteenth Street, N. W., Washington, D. C., 20036.

New Century Educational Division, Meridith Corp., 440 Park Avenue South, New York, New York, 10016.

New Readers Press, Division of Laubach Literacy, Inc., Box 131, Syracuse, New York, 13210.

New York Association for Brain Injured Children, 305 Broadway, New York, New York, 10007.

The New York Times, Book & Educational Division, 229 West 43rd Street, New York, New York, 10036.

New York University Press, Washington Square, New York, New York, 10003.

Henk Newenhouse, Inc., 1825 Willow Road, Northfield, Illinois, 60093.

Nicholas Books, Box 577, Williamstown, Massachusetts, 01267.

Noble & Noble Publishers, Inc., 750 Third Avenue, New York, New York, 10017.

A. J. Nystom & Co., 3333 North Elston Avenue, Chicago, Illinois, 60618.

O

The Oddo Publishing Co., Box 999, Mankato, Minnesota, 56002.

Office of Economic Opportunity, Washington, D. C., 20506.

Development Department, State of Ohio, 65 South Front Street, Box 1001, Columbus, Ohio, 43216.

Ohio & Michigan Paper Co., P. O. Box 621, Toledo, Ohio, 43601.

Ohio State Department of Education, Division of Special Education, 3201 Alberta Street, Columbus, Ohio, 43204.

Ohio Youth Commission, 2280 West Broad Street, Columbus, Ohio, 43223.

Open Court Publishing Co., Box 399, LaSalle, Illinois, 61301.

Optometric Extension Program Foundation, Inc., Duncan Oklahoma, 73533.

F. A. Owen Publishing Company, Instructo Park, Dansville, New York, 14437.

Oxford University Press, 200 Madison Avenue, New York, New York, 10016.

P

Paine Publishing Co., 34 North Jefferson Street, Dayton, Ohio, 45401.

Palfrey's School Supply Co., 7715 East Garvey Avenue, South San Gabriel, California, 91777.

Parents' Magazine Press, 52 Vanderbilt Avenue, New York, New York, 10017.

Parker Publishing Co., Inc., West Nyack, New York, 10994.

Parkinson Division, Follett Educational Corp., 1010 W. Washington Boulevard, Chicago, Illinois, 60607.

William E. Pedley, 5653 Dana Way, Sacramento, California, 95822.

Peek Publications, 4067 Transport Street, Palo Alto, California, 94303.

Pennsylvania State University Press, 215 Wagner Building, University Park, Pennsylvania, 16802.

Pergamon Press, 44-01 21st Street, Long Island City, New York, 11101.

Peripole, Inc., 51-17 Rockaway Beach Boulevard, Far Rockaway, New York, 11691.

Phonovisual Products, Inc., 4708 Wisconsin Avenue, Washington, D. C., 20016.

PESA, Box 292, Trumbull, Connecticut, 06606.

Pitman Publishing Corp., 20 East 46th Street, New York, New York, 10017.

University of Pittsburgh Press, Pittsburgh, Pennsylvania, 15213.

Playtime Equipment Co., 808 Howard Street, Omaha, Nebraska, 68102.

Plough Publishing House, Rifton, New York, 12471.

PM & E Electronics, Inc., P. O. Box 4263, East Providence, Rhode Island, 02914.

Pocket Books, Inc., Washington Square Press, Inc., 630 Fifth Avenue, New York, New York, 10020.

Popular Library, Inc., 355 Lexington Ave., New York, New York, 10017.

Portal Press, Inc., Publishers, 605 Third Avenue, New York, New York, 10016.

Port-aPit, Inc., P. O. Box C, Temple City, California, 91780.

Praeger Paperbacks, Frederick A. Praeger, Inc., Publishers, 111 Fourth Avenue, New York, New York, 10003.

Prentice-Hall, Inc., Education Book Division, Englewood Cliffs, New Jersey, 07632.

J. A. Preston Corp., 71 Fifth Avenue, New York, New York, 10003.

Pruett Press, Inc., 2930 Pearl Street, Box 1560, Boulder, Colorado, 80302.

The Psychological Corp., 304 East 45th Street, New York, New York, 10017.

Psychotechnics, Inc., 1900 Pickwick Avenue, Glenview, Illinois, 60025.

Publishers Central Bureau, 33-20 Hunters Point Avenue, Long Island City, New York, 11101.

G. P. Putman's Sons, 200 Madison Avenue, New York, New York, 10016.

Q

Quaker State Oil Refining Corp. Oil City, Pennsylvania.

Quality Products Co., 1816 N. W. 23rd Avenue, Portland Oregon.

Nate Quillen Instructional Systems 620 East Smith Road, Medina, Ohio, 44256.

R

Radiant Corporation, 8220 North Austin Avenue, Morton Grove, Illinois, 60053.

Rand McNally & Co., P. O. Box 7600, Chicago, Illinois, 60680.

Random House, Inc., Westminster, Maryland, 21157.
or
School & Library Service, 457 Madison Avenue, New York, New York, 10022.

Reader's Digest Services, Inc., Educational Division, Pleasantville, New York, 10570.

REA Express, 219 East 42nd Street, New York, New York, 10017.

Reinhold Book Corp., 430 Park Avenue, New York, New York, 10022.

Responsive Environments Corp. (R. E. C.), 200 Sylvan Avenue, Englewood Cliffs, New Jersey, 07632.

Frank E. Richards, Publisher, 215 Church Street, Phoenix, New York, 13135.

Richtext Press, 1224 W. Van Buren Street, Chicago, Illinois, 60607 (Division of Children's Press).

Ronald Press Co., 79 Madison Avenue, New York, New York, 10016.

S

S & S Arts & Crafts, Colchester, Connecticut, 06415 (Division of S & S Leather Co.).

W. H. Sadlier, Inc., 11 Park Place, New York, New York, 10007.

Howard W. Sams & Co., Inc., Publishers, 4300 West 62nd Street, Indianapolis, Indiana, 46268.

Porter Sargent, Publisher 11 Beacon Street, Boston, Massachusetts, 02108.

Sax Brothers, 207 N. Milwaukee, Milwaukee, Wisconsin, 53202.

Warren Schloat Productions, Inc., Pleasantville, New York, 10570.

Schocken Books, Inc., 67 Park Avenue, New York, New York, 10006.

Scholarly Books in America, Room 802-J, One Park Avenue, New York, New York, 10016.

Scholastic Magazines, Inc., 904 Sylvan Avenue, Englewood Cliffs, New Jersey, 07632.

Sci-Art Publishers, 35 Fenway Drive, Framingham, Massachusetts, 01701.

Science Research Associates, Inc., 259 East Erie Street, Chicago, Illinois, 60611.

Scott, Foresman & Co., 1900 East Lake Avenue, Glenview, Illinois, 60025.

Seating Engineering, 432 East Maple Avenue, P. O. Box 226, Miamisburg, Ohio, 45342.

The Seeing Eye, Inc., Morristown, New Jersey, 07960.

Selected Academis Readings. Division of Associated Educational Services Corp., 1 West 39th Street, New York, New York, 10020.

Selected Creative Communication, Box 1143, Santa Ana, California, 92702.

Shorewood Reproductions, 724 Fifth Avenue, New York, New York, 10019.

Sifo Co., 834 N. 7th Street, Minneapolis, Minnesota, 55411.

Silver Burdett Co., 460 S. Northwest Highway, Park Ridge, Illinois, 60068.

Simon & Schuster, Inc., Educational & Library Department, 630 Fifth Avenue, New York, New York, 10020.

L. W. Singer Co., Order Entry Department, Westminster, Maryland, 21157.

Dr. Skeen's Educational Aids, P. O. Box 8816, Denver Colorado, 80210.

Social Perceptual Products, 5927 Brookside Boulevard, Kansas City, Missouri, 64113.

Society for Visual Education, Inc., 1345 Diversey Parkway, Dept. 104, Chicago, Illinois, 60614 (Division of the Singer Co.).

Sound Materials, P. O. Box 453, Knoxville, Tennessee, 37901.

Special Child Publications, 71 Columbia Street, Room 320, Seattle, Washington, 98104.

Special Education Materials Developement Center (S.E.M.D.C.), 2020 "R" Street, N. W., Washington, D. C., 20009.

Speech & Language Materials, Inc., P. O. Box 721, Tulsa Oklahoma, 74101.

Speech Foundation of America, 150 Lombardy Road, Memphis, Tennessee, 38111.

Speech Materials, Box 1713, Ann Arbor, Michigan, 48106.

Spicewood Films, Inc., P. O. Box 9541, Austin, Texas, 78756.

Stanley Tools, 350 Fifth Avenue, New York, New York, 10020.

Stanwix House, Inc., 3020 Chartiers Avenue, Pittsburgh, Pennsylvania, 15204.

Steck-Vaughn Co., P. O. Box 2028, Austin, Texas, 78767.

Sterling Educational Films, 241 East 34th Street, New York, New York, 10016 (Division of Walter Reade Organization).

Sterling Publishing Co., Inc., 419 Park Avenue, South, New York, New York, 10016.

Stevens Foundation, Inc., 610-612 Endicott Building, St. Paul, Minnesota, 55101.

R. H. Stone Products, 18279 Livernois, Detroit, Michigan, 48221.

Gordon N. Stowe & Associates, P. O. Box 233-A, Northbrook, Illinois, 60062.

Summy-Birchard Co., 1834 Ridge Avenue,, Evanston, Illinois, 60204.

Sunkist Growers, Box 2706, Terminal Annex, Los Angeles, California, 90054.

Sunset House, 114 Sunset Building, Beverly Hills, California, 90213.

Swift & Co., Advertising Supply Department, 41st and S. Laflin Streets, Chicago, Illinois, 60609.

Systems for Education, Inc., 612 N. Michigan Avenue, Chicago, Illinois, 60611.

T

Mabel E. Talbot, Box-Books, 12 East South Street, Geneseo, New York, 14454.

Talens & Son, Inc., Union, New Jersey, 07083.

Taplinger Publishing Co., 29 East 10th Street, New York, New York, 10003.

Taylor Instrument, Consumer Products Division, Sybron Corp., Arden, North Carolina, 28704.

Taylor Publishing Co., P. O. Box 597, Dallas, Texas, 75221.

Teachers College Press, Teachers College, Columbia University, New York, New York, 10027.

Teachers Practical Press, Inc., 47 Frank Street, Valley Stream, New York, 11580.

Teachers Publishing Corp., 23 Leroy Avenue, Dairen, Connecticut, 06820.

Teaching Aids Company, 1609 West 29th Street, Davenport, Iowa, 52804.

Teaching Resources, 100 Boylston Street, Boston, Massachusetts, 02116.

Technicolor, Commercial & Educational Division, 1300 Frawley Drive, Costa Mesa, California, 92627.

Tecnifax Corp., Holyoke, Massachusetts.

Tepping Studio Supply Co., 3517 Riverside Drive, Dayton Ohio, 45405.

Texas Ass'n for Children with Learning Disabilities, Book Division, 1617 Fannin # 3009, Houston, Texas, 77002.

Charles C Thomas, Publisher, 301-327 East Lawrence Avenue, Springfield, Illinois, 62703.

Thorne Films Inc., 1229 University Avenue, Boulder, Colorado, 80302.

Time-Life Books, Time and Life Building, Chicago, Illinois, 60611.

Tok-Back, Inc., 2926 Avalon Avenue, Berkely, California, 94715.

Touch Aids, C. & E. Krueger, 1790 S. Juniper Street, Escondido, California, 92025.

Fern Tripp, 2035 East Sierra Way, Dinuba, California, 93618.

Tupperware International, Box 2353, Orlando, Florida, 32802.
   (or)

Kayette Sales, 229 "O" Street, Willis Day Industrial Park, Perrysburg, Ohio, 43551.

Turtox Laboratories, General Biological Supply House, Inc., 8200 S. Hoyne Avenue, Chicago, Illinois, 60620.

U

United Air Lines, P. O. Box 66141, O'Hare International Airport, Chicago, Illinois, 60666.

United Cerebral Palsy Association, Inc., 66 East 34th Street, New York, New York, 10016.

United Church Press, 1505 Race Street, Philadelphia, Pennsylvania, 19102.

United States Borax, 3075 Wilshire Boulevard, Los Angeles, California, 90005.

United States Department of Agriculture, Washington, D. C., 20250.

United States Department of Health, Education and Welfare, Office of Education, Washington, D. C., 20250.

United States Department of the Interior, Bureau of Reclamation, Office of Chief Engineer, Building 67, Denver Federal Center, Denver, Colorado, 80225.

United States Department of the Interior, Fish & Wildlife Service, Bureau of Commercial Fisheries, 1801 N. Moore Street, Arlington, Virginia, 22209.

United States Department of Justice, Federal Bureau of Investigation, Washington, D. C., 20535.

United States Government Printing Office, Superintendent of Documents, Washington, D. C., 20402.

United States Library of Congress, Division for the Blind and Physically Handicapped, 1291 Taylor Street, N. W., Washington, D. C., 20542.

United States National Commission for UNESCO, Department of State, United States of America, Washington, D. C., 20520.

United States Office of Education, Bureau for Education of Handicapped Children, Washington, D. C., 20202.

United World Films, Inc., Universal Education & Visual Arts, 221 Park Avenue South, New York, New York, 10003 (Division of Universal City Studios).

Urban Media Materials, P. O. Box 133, Flushing, New York, 11365.

V

D. Van Nostrand Co., Inc., 120 Alexander Street, Princeton, New Jersey, 08540.

Vega Products Division, Ameriplastic Co., Inc., G-5371 S. Saginaw Street, Flint, Michigan, 48507.

Viking Press, 625 Madison Avenue, New York, New York, 10022.

University of Virginia Hospital, Ronald Adams, Director, Recreational Therapy & Adaptive Physical Education, Children's Rehabilitation Center, Charlottesville, Virginia, 22901.

Visual Products, Division of 3M Co., 2501 Hudson Road, St. Paul, Minnesota, 55119.

W. J. Voit Rubber Corp., Santa Ana, California, 92702.

W

Wadsworth Publishing Co., Belmont, California, 94002.

Walden Film Corp., 39 E. 31st Street, New York, New York, 10016.

Lee Wards, 840 North State, Elgin, Illinois, 60120.

Jay L. Warren, Inc., 721 W. Belmont Avenue, Chicago, Illinois, 60657.

Franklin Watts, Inc., 575 Lexington Avenue, New York, New York, 10022.

Weber Costello, Division of Beckley-Cardy Co., 1900 N. Narragansett Avenue, Chicago, Illinois, 60639.

Westab Educational Services, (Mead Educational Services), 245 N. Highland Avenue, N. E., Atlanta, Georgia, 30307.

Western Interstate Commission for Higher Education, University East Campus, 30th Street, Boulder, Colorado, 80302.

Western Psychological Services, 12035 Wilshire Boulevard, Los Angeles, California, 90025.

Western Publishing Co., School & Library Department, 150 Parish Drive, Wayne, New Jersey, 07470.

Western Publishing Education, 1220 Mound Avenue, Racine, Wisconsin, 53404 (Division of Western Publishing Co.).

Western Wood Products Association, Yeon Building, Portland, Oregon, 97204.

Westinghouse Learning Corp., 100 Park Avenue, New York, New York, 10017.

Weston Woods, Weston, Connecticut, 06880.

Albert Whitman & Co., 560 West Lake Street, Chicago, Illinois, 60606.

INDEX